POINT OF
ORIGIN

"*Point of Origin* is not a book *about* Gobekli Tepe, but it sets that mysterious Anatolian hilltop sanctuary into a matrix of interconnected mysteries from all around the world in a way that is both fascinating and thought-provoking."

GRAHAM HANCOCK, AUTHOR OF *FINGERPRINTS OF THE GODS*

"*Point of Origin* is undoubtedly the pinnacle of research into the world's ancient cultures, their mysteries and mythologies . . . a truthful and accurate insight into our origins, encompassing religion, astronomy, mythology, and cosmology. This book is indispensable to anyone seeking answers about our origins."

E. A. JAMES SWAGGER, RADIO HOST AND AUTHOR OF
THE NEWGRANGE SIRIUS MYSTERY

"Learn the language of the Cosmos and explore the mysteries of Gobekli Tepe—the world's oldest civilization. Another fabulous book on ancient myths and symbols by one of the masters in the field."

XAVIANT HAZE, AUTHOR OF *ALIENS IN ANCIENT EGYPT*

"Once again Laird Scranton greatly expands our understanding of the ancient world through his relentless and meticulous research of language and symbol. This knowledge was to be preserved and passed down through the ages for a time in the future when the information would be vitally important for the survival of humanity. That time is now!"

EDWARD NIGHTINGALE, AUTHOR OF *THE GIZA TEMPLATE*

POINT OF ORIGIN

GOBEKLI TEPE AND THE SPIRITUAL MATRIX FOR THE WORLD'S COSMOLOGIES

LAIRD SCRANTON

Inner Traditions

Rochester, Vermont • Toronto, Canada

Inner Traditions
One Park Street
Rochester, Vermont 05767
www.InnerTraditions.com

Text stock is SFI certified

Library of Congress Cataloging-in-Publication Data
Scranton, Laird, 1953–
  Point of origin : Gobekli tepe and the spiritual matrix for the world's cosmologies / Laird Scranton.
     pages cm
  Includes bibliographical references and index.
  ISBN 978-1-62055-444-9 (pbk.) — ISBN 978-1-62055-445-6 (e-book)
  1. Turkey—Religion. 2. Göbekli Tepe (Turkey) 3. Mythology, Dogon. 4. Cosmology, Ancient. I. Title.
  BL1060.S37 2015
  939'.2—dc23

                                                              2014031366

Printed and bound in the United States by Lake Book Manufacturing, Inc.
The text stock is SFI certified. The Sustainable Forestry Initiative® program promotes sustainable forest management.

10 9 8 7 6 5 4 3 2 1

Text design and layout by Virginia Scott Bowman
This book was typeset in Garamond Premier Pro with Ulian, Copperplate Gothic, and Gill Sans used as display typefaces

To send correspondence to the author of this book, mail a first-class letter to the author c/o Inner Traditions • Bear & Company, One Park Street, Rochester, VT 05767, and we will forward the communication, or contact the author directly at **http://lairdscranton.com**.

Contents

Foreword

It's not every son who can say, "I watched my dad untie the secrets of the universe," but I'm proud to say that I can.

I was raised in an outwardly secular home by a Jewish/atheist mother and a convert father who sent me to a conservative/orthodox Jewish day school to learn the ins and outs of our extended family's tradition. I credit this seemingly self-contradictory childhood with fostering in me the ability to intelligently see and discuss subjects from more than one point of view, an ability that has uniquely qualified me to follow Laird's research from the very beginning. Later in life, as I rejected the dogmas that had been drilled into me in school, I began my own studies into comparative religion and philosophy. I practiced Zen meditation, examined the historical context of the New Testament, and compared the poetry and content of the Qur'an with the Dead Sea Scrolls and the Bhagavad Gita, and I soon came to see existence as a giant jigsaw puzzle, with each religious tradition holding a piece of it, but none holding the completed image.

Growing up, I took for granted my parents' endless collections of books, Buddha and Ganesha statues, and other esoteric paraphernalia. Not that Laird was particularly into esoteric study when I was a child; he wasn't. These collections were more artistic hobbies of his. Nonetheless, these images were comforting and familiar to me; they were more like old friends who'd been there for me for as long as I could remember. In hindsight, knowing now the work that would come to define Laird's later life, it seems almost like destiny that my family would already have an early connection to ancient ideas.

I was already proud to know that my father made his living as a self-employed software programmer, and it was not an uncommon occurrence for me as a young boy to sit at his side as he keyed in his billing hours to a program he'd written on our home computer and told me about sorting out the coded software messes he'd had to clean up for his clients that day. Knowing intimately his logical mind and his penchant for the unusual, it came as no real surprise when in my early days of high school, Laird announced that he'd stumbled on something fascinating in his pleasure reading about the Dogon tribe in Africa.

Now, as a child, I'd also grown up an avid fan of classic science fiction and fantasy, which in turn sparked a lifelong curiosity in me about the natural world and, in particular, physics; after all, what kid *doesn't* want to build a time machine at some point? A particular childhood favorite of mine was an animated television show called *The Mysterious Cities of Gold,* which chronicled the fictional adventures of a Spanish boy during the conquest of South America in the sixteenth century as he discovered remnants of Atlantean wonders sequestered away in the hidden temples and traditions of the native peoples. I'd bored my parents to death telling them the various details of each episode for ages. This little one-season show set the stage in my mind for the possibility that there was a wondrous advanced civilization that had come before our own and had been long forgotten. Imagine my surprise when it turned out that elements of this childhood favorite could actually be true!

As Laird's investigations grew to take on the air of a knight errant's holy quest, it seemed only too appropriate that I take on the proverbial role of squire, following his research, taking in his insights as he bounced them off of me, and occasionally helping him from my own knowledge to examine concepts in a new light when he found them difficult to understand. I was struck by how item after item that Laird uncovered seemed to tie into the various disciplines I studied on my own.

I soon realized that, while many could conceivably dismiss his investigations as the meaningless ravings of a pedantic amateur crackpot, the undeniable fact was that time and again his investigations not only reconciled religious conflicts in my mind, but they also demonstrably tied into hard science as well. The concepts he was discovering actually worked in practice!

Laird has conducted his work so that every step of the way he is focused on what he can demonstrate to be true. He doesn't make outlandish statements that he can't back up, no matter how much his audience may want him to. He sticks to what *is*, rather than what *could be*. Instead of simply falling back on the old "well, 'cause I say so" cop-out, he shows undeniably from multiple sources that what he says has a factual basis and that his conclusions are entirely logical. If he encounters something that doesn't agree across cultures or doesn't agree with what science can prove, he doesn't include it until he can show how it really connects.

This tells me that Laird is most certainly on the path toward something very real and very exciting, a system given all but uniformly to mankind in forgotten antiquity designed to transform us from mere beastly hunter-gatherers into a recognizable civilization and designed to be used a guidebook to taking us even further than we could imagine—in the material world as well as the spiritual.

Here is an ancient system that embraces everything at once. Like spiraling rays, each new strand that Laird finds ties together advanced science, astronomy, architecture, agriculture, religious rituals, and mysticism, and brings them all back to a central point. As, on my own, I study the more fashionable new age ideas presented in alchemy, Kabbalah, Zen, and Sufism, I continually find myself referring to the detailed notes and drafts of Laird's books to explain concepts that I find difficult to grasp. More often than not, Laird's explanation helps push me along in the right direction.

I often feel like someone rereading a Dan Brown novel, for I have the pleasure of already knowing how the mystery ends and get to see how well the author really puts the clues together. I realize, looking up at the stars or under a microscope, it's all one and the same. What happens in the skies above also happens within our cells below.

Now, after nearly twenty years of squiring for my father, I see his system everywhere I turn. I see it in the architecture of the Vatican, in Native American dances, in Jewish liturgy, in works of art, and in the latest discoveries from the European Organization for Nuclear Research (CERN). I see the triple domes of the Sakti goddesses at every church I pass. Through my studies of the public statements and symbolism of the Freemasons, I continue to see reflections back to Giza and Gobekli Tepe. The few times I still go to synagogue, I'm tickled at the invocation of an ancient deity's name to establish agreement after every prayer, and like the commandment states, it's never used in vain! Another side effect is that I now see Disney movies, with their emphasis on mice acting to remove the obstacles in our lives, in a whole new light (and in the case of *Dumbo,* we literally have a retelling of the major themes of Ganesha—the mother's elephant son, cast out and reborn, and being carried to glory by the efforts of a mouse).

The names often change, but the stories remain the same. Finally, I have a guide by which to complete the great jigsaw puzzle of existence!

When we consider the vast questions that concern the modern world—the proper role of religion in our lives, the impact of new scientific and technological advancement, how to implement the proper stewardship of the environment in a time of climate change, when and how life begins, who we are, and where we're going with one another—the importance of Laird's work cannot be understated. Not only does it reconcile ages of religious disagreement, establishing the common foundations of Islam, Judaism, Hinduism, Buddhism, Christianity, and the Tao, but it all relates back again to actual science! This system, so elegant in its simplicity yet so complex in its meaning, can put our species back onto a proper footing to move us all forward into a great future.

What we have in this work is nothing less than a unified system of everything that can reconcile science and mysticism, dogma and history, mathematics and faith—all in the most accessible, benevolent, and familiar of ways. It can point us, as it did eons ago for our primordial ancestors, toward our next level of development as a species.

As I've seen with my own eyes, Laird's work can—and will—illuminate our hearts and point our souls once again to the stars.

There can be no greater pleasure for a son.

ISAAC SCRANTON

Isaac Scranton is a stage director and actor in New York City, where he splits his time between directing in Indie Theatre and acting for the Metropolitan Opera. He is a featured, non-singing performer and stage fighter at the Met Opera, most notably in Mary Zimmerman's production of *Armida* and in *Manon*. In 2008, he received an OBIE Award for his work in The Living Theatre's revival of Ken Brown's *The Brig*. As a private supplement to Laird's research, Isaac has extensively studied the symbols and myths of many traditions, including Alchemy, Rosicrucianism, Kabbalah, Sufism, Tao, and Zen Buddhism. An avid follower of American history and politics, Isaac's writings on the state of the U.S.A. can be found at his blog, The Fed-Up Progressive.

Introduction

This volume is the fifth in a series of books whose focus is on concepts of ancient cosmology and language. The terms *cosmology* and *language* refer to the ways in which ancient cultures conceived of the processes of creation and to the words, myths, and symbols they used to express those concepts. From the perspective of many ancient societies, the term *cosmology* was applied somewhat more broadly than we might expect it to be today; for them the term commonly referred to the processes by which the universe, our material world, and humanity itself were thought to have come into existence. Because of this, our discussions of ancient cosmology have touched on subjects that range from folklore, myth, and religion to biology, astronomy, and even astrophysics.

In this series of volumes, our studies began with a modern-day African tribe called the Dogon, whose culture reflects many of the archetypal elements that we associate with the classic ancient creation traditions from Africa, Egypt, India, and Asia. To have encountered such a broad set of symbols, themes, words, and concepts coexisting side by side within a single culture suggested that these ancient traditions may have once shared more of a common history than has been traditionally presumed. This presented us with a unique opportunity to explore a broad set of potential commonalities among those seemingly distinct traditions. My approach throughout these studies has been to compare the beliefs and practices of several different ancient traditions as a way to learn more about them, and so the field of study they relate to is appropriately called *comparative cosmology*. Such comparative studies rest on the use of certain techniques that help us to correlate different aspects of these ancient traditions in positive ways.

In the prior volumes of this series, my discussion has shown that the words of Dogon cosmology are arguably ancient Egyptian words. We discovered that the Dogon cosmology presents a very close match for an ancient Buddhist tradition, although the two systems are given in outwardly different languages. I now understand that important Dogon ritual practices have existed since ancient times in the Judaic tradition and that many of the cosmological words of the Dogon and Egyptian cultures also existed in similar form in the comparably ancient Hebrew language. Moreover, I was able to demonstrate that attributes shared by these first three traditions served to accurately predict what I would later find when I explored the creation tradition and hieroglyphic language of an ancient Tibetan tribe called the Na-Khi (or Na-Xi). These same attributes also proved to be predictive when I examined the sometimes poorly understood words and traditions of ancient China.

Any researcher of ancient mystery traditions relies on interpreted meanings to arrive at an understanding of the material he or she studies. Unfortunately, the human psyche is arguably "wired" to infer patterns and meanings in an otherwise confused world, sometimes even in situations where those meanings may not actually pertain. For instance, what young child hasn't looked up to the sky and marveled at images he or she perceived in random cloud shapes? In my experience, one of the great professional dangers to those who study ancient traditions lies somewhere in the dark recesses of their own subconscious wishfulness. This danger can take the form of subtle predispositions that lead us to perceive a pattern where none actually exists or to draw inferences that are objectively unwarranted.

This is not to say that resemblances are not an essential part of the process of ancient studies, because in my view they surely are. In fact, the search for new interpretations may often begin with the simple suggestion of a resemblance that the researcher chooses to pursue, hoping to decipher whether the similarity is more likely the product of coincidence or of overt intention. In any case, I believe it is the essential job of the researcher to demonstrate that any perceived resemblance is not merely a wishful one. In order to guard against my own wishful tendencies, I have tried to adopt a professional standard: that whenever possible, each interpretation should begin with an overt statement on the part of the culture being studied and this statement should either be overtly confirmed by references from other similar cultures or else be clearly restated in more than one way within the first culture.

My view is that in order to successfully sustain an interpreted argument, it is the researcher's obligation at each stage of the discussion to supply a straightforward ending to a single sentence: "We know this must be true because . . ." The simpler the formulation of that sentence, the more defensible the argument will ultimately prove to be. If the researcher can satisfy this requirement, then whether or not a critic agrees with the author's perspective, the interpretation should still be seen as justifiable. If for some reason the researcher is unable to satisfy the sentence, then for me the interpretation may simply lack foundation.

The primary reference books I rely on when making comparisons of ancient traditions are the works of Marcel Griaule and Germaine Dieterlen, two French anthropologists who conducted a series of expeditions among the Dogon over a period of nearly three decades, ending in 1956. Foremost among these books are Griaule's *Conversations with Ogotemmeli* (a diary of his instruction as a Dogon initiate) and Griaule and Dieterlen's definitive study of the Dogon religion, *The Pale Fox*. My comparisons to ancient Buddhist traditions begin with a book called *The Symbolism of the Stupa* by Adrian Snodgrass of the

University of Western Sydney in Australia. The stupa is an aligned ritual shrine whose plan and symbolism are a close match for those of an important Dogon shrine, referred to as a granary. Snodgrass has written on a broad range of subjects relating to Buddhism and is widely seen as a leading authority on Buddhist architecture and symbolism.

Correlations between Dogon and Egyptian words are made based on two dictionaries. The first is the *Dictionnaire Dogon,* a French dictionary of the Dogon language compiled by Marcel Griaule's daughter, Genevieve Calame-Griaule, who came to be an accomplished and respected anthropologist in her own right. The second is Sir E. A. Wallis Budge's *An Egyptian Hieroglyphic Dictionary,* an early-twentieth-century dictionary of the Egyptian hieroglyphic language. I fully understand that my choice to use this dictionary could be problematic for some traditional Egyptologists, many of whom strongly disagree with Budge's outlook on the Egyptian hieroglyphic language. However, the obscure body of Dogon cosmological words, which may be largely unfamiliar to these Egyptian language scholars, also provides me with a rare independent cross-check on Budge's own pronunciations and meanings, especially as regards ancient words of cosmology. Throughout my studies in ancient cosmology, I have found Budge's dictionary to be in close agreement with Dogon usage as it was meticulously documented by Griaule, Dieterlen, and Calame-Griaule. I take this body of well-defined Dogon cosmological words and their consistent correspondence to Budge's work as a practical demonstration of the soundness of Budge's dictionary.

These primary reference sources, together with others that I will introduce as we proceed, will allow us to effectively triangulate the likely meanings of the ancient cosmological words, concepts, and themes that we will study. To the extent that the sources are in agreement with one another regarding the underlying meanings of any given term, symbol, or concept, we can feel confident in putting those meanings forward as an informed interpretation.

I should note that a restudy of Griaule's work was conducted in the 1980s by Belgian anthropologist Walter Van Beek. Van Beek and his team reported that, over the course of a few years of study, they were unable to find outward evidence of the system of Dogon cosmological beliefs that Griaule had described as a closely held secret tradition. Based on that result, Van Beek concluded that the tradition must have been fabricated by obliging Dogon priests for Griaule's benefit. However, Van Beek and other later Dogon researchers who followed Griaule somehow missed the many abiding Dogon parallels to the Buddhist stupa tradition that would seem to lend legitimacy and coherence to the system of cosmology Griaule described. Many of the details reported by Griaule constitute what I call "privileged knowledge" of the Buddhist tradition and reflect information that should not have been known to Griaule except after many focused years of study in Buddhism, work that Griaule's biographers fail to report him as ever having actually made. Moreover, to my knowledge none of these parallels to Buddhism were ever noted or commented on by any of Griaule's team or by any other Dogon researcher for more than sixty years following Griaule's death in 1956. My outlook is that the parallelism of the Buddhist references upholds the legitimacy of Griaule's Dogon cosmology and suggests that Van Beek's team simply failed to penetrate what Griaule characterized as a well-kept secret tradition.

The origin of the classic ancient creation traditions is one of the great unanswered mysteries of human history. In fact, it quickly becomes clear to those who study it that any search for credible answers to this mystery must extend far back beyond the beginnings of actual written history. We know that many of the longstanding symbols and concepts preserved in these traditions preceded the earliest evidence of written language in any given culture, for example, that reverence for a Neith-like mother goddess, and of primordial mother goddesses in general, dates to Neolithic times—or as one reference puts it, to "time immemorial." This does not mean, however, that we are without recourse when it comes to attempting to discover many of the ultimate roots of these traditions, only that the methods we employ as we work our way conceptually backward in time may require ever-greater ingenuity if we hope to continue to extract useful information from ever-slimmer sets of evidence.

Until now, the focus of my studies has been on an era that dates from around 3000 BCE, which is the point in human development when systems of writing were first adopted and when organized civic centers made their earliest appearance. However, my intention in this volume is to explore relationships that I believe must extend much further back in time, perhaps to a period thousands of years before the first surviving written text. I know based on my discussions of ancient Chinese cosmology in *China's Cosmological Prehistory,* the previous volume of this series, that lack of written evidence can place my arguments on a somewhat different footing, that without such evidence to rely on, I may not always expect to find overt confirmation for every observation I make. Therefore when formulating my arguments in this volume, I may sometimes be required to place more emphasis on the powers of inference or of informed supposition than I have in prior volumes.

As I noted in *The Science of the Dogon,* it is to the benefit of my studies that even over long periods of time, words tend not to leave the language of a culture, especially words that are known to carry heightened significance, as words of cosmology often do. In the parlance of modern linguists, terms such as these are referred to as *ultraconserved words.* For example, we know that, four hundred years later, many of the words and phrases that Shakespeare used still appear in modern English usage, if perhaps now in a form that is considered to be somewhat quaint or archaic. The same is especially true for words and phrases that come down to us through the auspices of religion, where revered writings tend to be carefully preserved or copied forward and passed down. For example, thousands of years later it is still commonly understood that the phrase "to know," taken in the biblical sense, refers to an act of procreation. In a similar way, we can use archaic Egyptian word forms, or ancient words that survive in the modern-day languages of other cultures, to learn more about preliterate concepts that define cosmology.

Although it can only be called an unorthodox approach, another observation that works to our advantage when pursuing symbolic references that predate written language is the high degree of commonality of words that I have observed to exist among very ancient traditions. In fact, my experience has been that the further back in time I go, the more commonality of language I ultimately find. I was able to exploit this apparent feature of ancient language in my previous discussions of ancient Tibetan and Chinese cosmological terms, many of which align well with both Dogon and ancient Egyptian words. Often these resemblances allowed me to refine my understanding of a poorly understood ancient word by comparing it to similar but more explicitly defined words found in the Dogon and Egyptian dictionaries.

At this point in my studies, the obvious outward language differences that are evident between the Dogon and Buddhist cosmological traditions work as a benefit to my interpretations, rather than a detriment. On one level, this is because the substantial differences argue that neither culture likely received its tradition directly from the other, but rather that each acquired its own cosmology from some common, preexisting source. This observation allows me to safely infer that neither the Buddhists nor the Dogon priests have simply perpetuated the others' wishful misperceptions or misremembrances, but rather that they each proactively confirm each others' stated outlook. Consequently, whenever the Dogon and Buddhist traditions demonstrate agreement about a particular subject, I can argue that it rises to the level of corroborated testimony, not mutually shared ignorance.

Likewise, the very close similarity of the Dogon and Egyptian cosmological words confirms that the Dogon meanings and pronunciations cannot have wandered terribly far from the mark over time, since any contact between the Dogon and the Egyptians must have taken place many thousands of years ago. A nineteenth-century researcher of esoteric religions named Samuel Johnson (not to be confused with the well-known eighteenth-century compiler of dictionaries by the same name) wrote, "The Word has always been recognized as the fittest symbol of truth, as the purest manifestation of deity. This unimpeachable witness it is, that testifies of man in an antiquity where no other is possible."[1]

1

The Ancient Cosmological/ Civilizing Plan

Over the course of the four previous books of this series, We have discussed a number of cultures whose creation traditions appear to be fundamentally similar to one another. These include the cultures of the modern-day Dogon tribe of Mali, the ancient Egyptians, the ancient Buddhists, the Tibetan Na-Khi tribe, and the ancient Chinese. In each of these cultures there is an abiding belief that civilizing skills relating to agriculture, weaving, pottery, metallurgy, stone masonry, the domestication of animals, and written language—among others—were intentionally given to humanity in some remote era by knowledgeable, quasi-mythical ancestor-teachers or ancestor-deities. Each culture we have studied closely associates these instructed civilizing skills with important concepts of their creation tradition (or cosmology). The purpose of this instructed civilizing plan is understood by the most knowledgeable initiates of these cultures to have been to raise humanity upward from the status of hunter-gatherers to that of farmers. From a similar perspective, the Dogon priests assert that one of the foremost purposes of the cosmology was to help mankind understand our own place within the larger processes of creation.

The close association of the civilizing plan with the concepts of cosmology in these traditions, along with our need to relate the two, could create potentially cumbersome terminology for the purposes of this study. References given in relation to one of these two concepts often also have meaning in relation to the other. To ease that difficulty, our choice within this volume will be to use the terms *creation tradition, cosmology,* and *civilizing plan* as largely interchangeable terms, each referring to what the Dogon broadly describe as an ancestral religio-cultural-cosmological system, but with emphasis on the specific aspect of that system under discussion.

During our discussions in previous volumes of this series we developed a list of features commonly exhibited by these ancient creation traditions that we referred to as *signature signs* of the cosmology; these are attributes that, if they were to be found among the traditions of some other, less-familiar culture, would signal the likely influence of this same cosmological plan. These attributes are the subject of discussion in *The Cosmological Origins of Myth and Symbol.* Rather than simply recount these signature attributes again here, it is our intention in this volume to take an alternate approach: to simply entertain the Dogon and Buddhist belief that these correlated cosmologies were intentionally instructed and to attempt to frame a sensible rationale within which to understand that belief.

Because the Dogon have a living culture and are known to place a high value on the correctness of their tradition and word usage, their priests offer us the clearest overall picture of how this plan of ancient cosmology may have been originally structured. Given the signs of their early relationship with ancient Egypt, the Dogon also present what is arguably our most ancient window into this ancient plan. Over time, however, as with the long-term traditions of any culture, some aspects of that plan certainly may have fallen by the wayside. We see indications that this has happened even among the Dogon, where, for example, only passing reference is made to the symbolic concept of a mulberry tree, but without the kind of supporting details we find in ancient China, and so the Dogon reference gives the appearance of a lost thread. Conversely, we are told of a "theoretical" ancient agricultural plan in China called the well-field system that overtly matches actual practices that define agriculture among the Dogon. These parallels suggest that the ancient Chinese plan may have, in fact, been somewhat more than simply theoretical. It is the goal of the comparative cosmologist to discover and learn from these types of differences in cultural outlook. Consequently, any inferences we make regarding an ancient shared plan of cosmology must necessarily consider the stated viewpoints of various traditions.

The notion of "ancestors" is one that plays a very visible role in each of the traditions we have studied, and it is reflected in an anthropological concept called ancestor worship. In the traditional academic view, the notion of ancestor worship among early cultures is often treated like a kind of primitive precursor to modern concepts of religion, whereas in relation to the traditions we study, the concept of an "ancestor" plays an important cosmological role. Like other key concepts associated with the civilizing plan, the term *ancestor* carries more than one definition. From the perspective of everyday life, the word embodies the Dogon sense of their own lineage, which is understood in terms of the descent of eight ancestral families, each having originated with one of eight mythical Dogon ancestors.

One common assertion made by various cultures that share this tradition is that civilizing instruction was actually given to humanity indirectly and, for the most part, not by the theoretical authors of the civilizing plan themselves. For example, the Dogon priests believe that select members of their tribe were taken away to a remote locale for instruction and then returned home again, in order to pass on their newly acquired knowledge to their compatriots. From an instructional perspective, the Dogon term *ancestors* often refers to these intermediary tribe members, who were seen as bringers of ancestral knowledge. The name of one of the mythical Dogon ancestors, Lebe, suggests a possible linkage to a similar concept in Judaism, where a family or tribal lineage called Levi is still retained and honored. Likewise, there is a class of Dogon priests called the Hogon, a term that calls to mind a comparable Jewish priestly class called the Cohain.

Within the structure of their cosmology, symbolic Dogon

"ancestors" often hold places or define mythic concepts in ways that can be compared to those of named deities in other cultures, such as those of ancient Egypt or India. For example, during discussion of the processes of creation, Dogon "ancestors" are said to have emerged in male/female pairs, similar to the eight paired Egyptian Ennead or Ogdoad gods and goddesses. As a rule, where the Dogon myths define ancestors or ancestor-teachers, the ancient Egyptians and the Vedic-based religions of India define gods or ancestor-gods.

From another Dogon perspective, the term *ancestor* seems to refer to mythical teachers who are said to have originally designed the civilizing plan. If there has been one constant we have seen regarding the ancient traditions we have studied, it is that the mythical ancestor-teachers credited with formulating this plan seem at all times to have had the very best interests of an emerging humanity at heart. The factual meanings that attach to the symbols and myths of these traditions appear to reflect a correct, informed understanding of the actual processes of nature. Likewise, the civilizing plan itself includes elements that, in my view, are consistently reflective of careful and conscientious design.

There are many factors to suggest that the Dogon creation tradition must be an ancient one. First, as their use of the term *ancestor* suggests, the tradition is aniconic, which means (among other things) that it is not the Dogon practice to create personified images of their deities, as the Egyptians are known for doing. In truth, the Dogon only recognize one mythical personage (their creator-god Amma), who could be said to rise to the level of an actual deity in the Egyptian sense of the word, and the Dogon are not generally known to depict Amma anthropomorphically in their art. Also, in the traditions we study there is a general progression from very archaic, aniconic forms to a more recent era when deities were routinely personified and depicted in ancient art. Second, although the Dogon place a very high value on the purity of language, they have no native written language of their own, a fact that strongly suggests that they never actually had one. Likewise, although the Dogon observe the same calendar systems as the ancient Egyptians, they make no reference to the system of five intercalary days that was known to have existed in ancient Egypt. These are both attributes that are believed to have appeared quite early in Egyptian history, and so the fact that they are not found to exist with the Dogon implies that any face-to-face association between the two cultures is likely to have happened quite early in Egyptian history.

If so, then such an early period of contact implies that we should also find commonalities between Dogon culture and that of the North African Amazigh tribes (ancestors to the modern-day Berbers), who resided in Egypt prior to the First Dynasty. In practice, that is just what we do find. For example, it is well documented that the Dogon share many words in common with these tribes. It is also generally agreed that the Egyptian mother goddess Neith was celebrated in predynastic times. Our studies have shown that, like the Dogon, the Amazigh observed a little-known esoteric tradition in which priestly titles were based on a root word that refers to "light" or "enlightenment."

The way in which Dogon cosmological references are structured suggests a reason why so many complexities seem to arise in the study of ancient symbolism. There are three distinct creational themes defined within the Dogon creation tradition that are conceptualized in parallel with one another. These are: (1) the creation of the universe, (2) the creation of matter, and (3) the creation of life through the processes of biological reproduction. All three themes are explained by the Dogon priests in relation to a single set of carefully defined symbols that are meant to serve all three themes concurrently. A typical Dogon symbol carries meanings that relate to each of the three parallel themes. For the purposes of this study, our references will be given primarily in relation to the creation of matter, because that theme offers the greatest number of discrete stages to be associated with the symbols.

Dogon definitions for these symbols are often given in distinctly scientific terms and may be paired with drawings that resemble appropriate scientific diagrams for the same concepts. So an egg, which constitutes one of the entry points both for the Dogon biological theme of creation and for biological reproductive science, is also given as an initiating image in relation to the formation of the universe and of matter. Parallelism of this type allows the Dogon priests to effectively declare a symbol once and then use its definition many times. The first obvious benefit that these Dogon references provide us with, in terms of the comparative cosmologies we have been pursuing, consists of clear, overt defining statements on which to base many of my interpretations. The second benefit comes from the coherent progression of concepts that we can understand the symbols to reflect, a structure that appears to be scientific and is therefore easy to follow, predict, and validate.

In each of the cultures we will study, there is evidence that the cosmology was meant to be a privileged esoteric system, meaning that only the most sincere and persistent of initiates would eventually master the innermost secrets of the tradition. However, it is also clear based on the Dogon model that the choice to pursue initiation was ultimately open to any interested person, Dogon or otherwise. Support for this outlook is found in Marcel Griaule's own personal experience as an outsider to the tribe who, because he pursued knowledge in a sincere and orderly fashion, was both initiated into the tradition by the Dogon priests and ultimately declared a Dogon citizen. After his death in 1956 Griaule was actually granted a Dogon burial. All of this implies that the ultimate rationale behind the esoteric nature of the tradition was not to maintain secrecy within the Dogon tribe or even from well-intentioned outsiders, but rather to secure a body of privileged knowledge from nameless outsiders who might not be so well intentioned.

For Dogon tribe members, initiation begins at birth and is first introduced through myths that are shared with the community at large. These myths are treated like instructive stories that are told around a campfire at night. Unlike the more familiar Greek and Roman myths that center largely on interpersonal intrigue among a family of gods and goddesses, the storylines of Dogon myths serve primarily to illustrate concepts of nature, to introduce certain broad cosmological themes and images, and to establish symbolic associations that will prove to be important to an initiate who chooses to study the creation tradition. For example, these stories describe how, at the time of creation, a primordial egg opened and cast pellets of clay throughout the universe. The Dogon myths define the sun as a clay pot that has been raised to a high heat and describe the moon as being a clay body that is dry and dead. They talk about water, its various states (liquid, frozen, and water vapor), and attributes of water in nature, such as its relationship to a mythical "perfect twin pair" called the Nummo. (When looked at scientifically, this last reference suggests the pair of hydrogen atoms that combine, along with an atom of oxygen, to form a water molecule.) They tell about a mythical celestial ram who is identified with the colors of the rainbow, who moves among the clouds, and whose body parts seem to symbolize various stages of the natural water cycle.

Any good parent with a child who is too young to fully understand the complexities of adult concepts learns to carefully frame the answers to certain questions like, "Where do babies come from?" The parent knows that he or she can only give a partial answer to this type of question when it is posed by a very young child. However, most parents also realize that any answer they do give should serve to properly orient the child to the more precise details he or she will someday learn. So it is understandable that a theoretical group of ancient instructors charged with the task of framing a creation tradition for a youthful humanity would have seen the wisdom in formulating it in terms of real science. It also makes sense within such a tradition that an introductory set of more generalized answers regarding questions of creation be offered for the benefit of the uninitiated, framed in such a way as to lead a young, curious person to seek more complete, precise answers.

In support of the scientific aspects of the tradition, the Dogon belief is that their cosmology describes, among other things, how a tribal god named Amma created the universe and matter. Although Griaule is careful to state that there is no single mythic narrative that defines this tradition, there are well-formed mythic storylines that relate certain key aspects of it. For example, the Dogon myths talk about a character

named Ogo, who thinks he can create a world as perfect as the one created by the Dogon god Amma. Ogo decides to break off a square piece
of Amma's "placenta" and from that piece evokes the material universe
that we perceive. One unforeseen outcome of this act is that it causes
Ogo to become separated from his twin sister and condemns him for-
ever to search for her but never to actually find her.

Like the Buddhists, the Dogon priests consider our material universe to be an illusion—the mere shadow, image, or reflection of a more
fundamental, underlying reality. Based on their descriptions, the process by which this image is evoked works in much same way that electri-
cal impulses that travel along a cable, or waves that have been broadcast
through the air, produce the picture we see on our television sets. They
exist in a wavelike state until the moment we cause them to be translated into a discrete image. However, the Dogon do also say that our
illusory universe represents a correct image of that more fundamental,
underlying reality.

One purpose of the first book of this series, *The Science of the
Dogon,* was to illustrate, through simple side-by-side comparison, the
reasonable correspondence of Dogon concepts of creation to modern
concepts of atomic theory, quantum theory, and string theory. String
theory proposes that matter is the product of microscopic strings, whose
vibrations we perceive as particles of matter, much as we interpret certain sound vibrations as musical tones. Each unique vibration of these
strings defines what we consider to be a different fundamental particle
of matter. It became clear to me during my studies that Dogon descriptions of these strings most closely resemble a controversial version of
string theory called torsion theory.

From the Dogon perspective, matter exists in three conceptual
worlds. It begins within the First World as waves in a perfectly ordered,
primordial state that for the Dogon priests represents the true essence
of existence. Each of the classic cosmologies we will study (along with
many modern religions) overtly claims that creation begins with water.
For the Dogon, any act of perception causes the perfect order of the

First World to become disrupted and initiates a process of reorganization that defines the Second World. This Second World corresponds to the microcosm of our reality. The Dogon associate the relative disorder of this world symbolically with a jackal, the same mythical animal that relates to the Egyptian underworld. The Dogon priests define our familiar material universe as the Third World of matter and, like the Vedics and Buddhists, consider it to be merely a reflected image of a more fundamental underlying reality.

The Dogon priests are in agreement with modern astrophysicists when they say that matter begins as waves and is then transformed by an act of perception into what we perceive as particles. The Dogon attribute this transformation to a series of seven vibrations that cause the matter in its wavelike state to draw up and repeatedly encircle. This process ultimately culminates in a rudimentary component of matter that the Dogon priests call "the egg of the world," a conceptual counterpart to a fundamental structure of string theory called the Calabi-Yau space. Astrophysicists conceive of this structure as a kind of bundle of collapsed dimensions that are thought to exist at every point in space and time. Based on Dogon descriptions, these "eggs" are essentially bubbles of mass or matter, consisting of a series of smaller bubbles that were too insubstantial to support their own weight. Each egg is conceived of by the Dogon priests in two alternate ways, first as a series of seven rays of a star of increasing length that radiate out from a central point, and next in terms of the imagined spiral that can be drawn to inscribe the endpoints of those radiating rays.

Light, mass, and primordial particles of matter called quarks are among the by-products of this transformation, along with four primordial forces: gravity, the electromagnetic force, the weak nuclear force (the force that binds larger particles like protons and neutrons together), and the strong nuclear force (the force that binds particles tightly together in the nucleus of an atom). For the Dogon these component processes of matter culminate in an atom-like structure called the *po,* from which all material things are made. Another African tribe called the Bambara, who Griaule and Dieterlen feel are related to the Dogon and who share a similar cosmology, conceptualize this egg in an alternate way. In the view of the Bambara, this egg of the world consists of seven straw-like filaments of increasing length, and it is the incremental spaces between the straws that are defined as rays of light.[1]

The Dogon priests offer careful definitions for each component stage of this transformational process and often frame their definitions in relation to a cosmological drawing. Many times these drawings reflect shapes that can actually be observed in nature, and so correspond to a special class of symbolic images that are referred to in Buddhism as "adequate symbols," defined as symbols that would retain their meanings even if the trail of symbolism were somehow lost to later generations of initiates of the tradition. For example, the likely Dogon counterparts to protons, neutrons, and electrons, called "sene seeds," are associated with a drawing that is a close match for one of the recognizable patterns created by an electron as it orbits the nucleus of an atom. This is a shape that can be directly imaged using an electron microscope, and so could be recognized by a capable society, independent of the symbolic tradition. These descriptions and drawings define a process of creation for matter that easily lends itself to correlation to modern scientific theory.

As part of the civilizing plan, the daily acts of Dogon life were structured in ways that symbolically reflected important processes of cosmological creation. For example, an archaic Dogon land-use system that called for agricultural plots to be laid out in the form of a spiral mimicked one conceptualization of the egg of the world. Once established, these symbolic associations created a kind of symbiotic correspondence between everyday acts of Dogon life and important cosmological processes whose net effect was to reinforce the cosmological teachings. As another example, the four conceptual stages involved in the construction of a building, beginning with its initial plan and ending with its final physical construction, define a kind of generic pattern or four-stage metaphor that is equated symbolically with four progressive stages of creation. Like all good definitions within the tradition, this metaphor is restated in several different ways as it is applied to the various creative themes of the tradition. The metaphors provide an external point of reference to which an initiate can refer when considering the proper relational sequence of various Dogon symbols.

An example of this kind of metaphor that would perhaps be most familiar to a modern audience is expressed in terms of the four classic elements of water, fire, wind, and earth. From the standpoint of the creation of matter it is clear these symbolize (respectively) matter in its underlying wavelike form, the act of perception that induces a primordial wave to be reorganized into particles, the concept of vibration that is credited as the source of this mysterious transformation, and the concept of mass or matter, which is an end product of the transformation. At a more generalized level of interpretation, these elements can also be seen to represent four distinct states of matter—liquid, plasma, gas, and solid. Considered in relation to this four-stage metaphor, any Dogon mythical reference that is given in terms of "water" is understood to refer to one of the initiating processes of creation, just as any reference to "earth" relates to one of the culminating processes. Essentially, the metaphor allows us to "place" symbolic references in the proper stage of a particular creational theme.

Within the plan of the cosmology, great care seems to have been taken to help us perceive and validate the meanings that lie behind ancient symbolic references, and so no concept seems to have been expressed in only one symbolic way. In fact, it may be more accurate to say that the plan of the cosmology all but hits us over the head with alternate symbolic formulations for its most important concepts, as if to assure that, no matter from what perspective we might approach the subject, we ultimately "get the message." So a series of different four-stage metaphors, all formulated similarly to the progression of water, fire, wind, and earth, seem to have been defined.

One of these metaphors is given in terms of the animal kingdom, and it begins with insects, then moves to fish, then to four-legged (or domesticated) animals, and finally to birds. This metaphor can be seen to define an upward progression of creatures from those that live in the water to those that crawl at ground level, to creatures that stand on legs, and finally to creatures that fly in the sky. (Insects such as the dung beetle, which represent the earliest state of existence in the Dogon and Egyptian cosmologies, are considered by the Dogon to be water beetles and so are associated with water in the Dogon tradition.) The familiar Egyptian animal-headed deities would seem to be an expression of this same cosmological metaphor, wherein the beetle-headed Kheper represents the concept of nonexistence coming into existence (an early stage of creation), the four-legged Anubis guards the underworld (a secondary stage), and the bird-headed Thoth is associated with completed words and language (the final stage of creation).

Another of these alternate Dogon metaphors is given in terms of the life cycle of a single animal (in this case, a goose). The metaphor progresses from an egg to a young gosling, to a standing goose, then to a flying goose. Again, the four stages of the metaphor can be seen to define a progression that moves conceptually upward.

Another comparable metaphor is given in terms of the plant kingdom. It begins with a seed and progresses to a new shoot, then to a young sapling, and finally to a grown plant. Again, the progressive stages of the metaphor define a process that moves conceptually upward.

Yet another of these metaphoric progressions is given in terms of the formation of a spoken or written word. This sequence begins with a "sign" (which can be taken to represent either a spoken phonetic value or a written character), then continues with the notion of "breath" (the vehicle of the spoken word or the implied motion associated with a drawn character), then with the concept of "vibration" (which can represent either the concept of a sound or the scribble associated with an act of writing), and culminates with the formation of a finished "Word."

The initial generic metaphor that was given in terms of the stages of a construction project also defines a series of cosmological terms to be associated with the four stages of each metaphor. We interpret these terms based on reconciled meanings of correlated Dogon and Egyptian words. The first (the stage in which the basic plan for the building to be constructed is laid out by marking out endpoints on the ground with stones) is called *bummo* by the Dogon. This word is a likely correlate to the Egyptian compound term *bu maa,* which means "to examine or perceive."[2] Symbolically, we interpret the Egyptian term to read "place perceived." The Dogon refer to the second stage of construction (when major features of the structure are further delineated on the ground with the placement of additional stones) as *yala,* meaning "mark" or "image." This term relates to the Egyptian word *ahau,* meaning "delimitation posts or boundaries."[3] The third stage (which represents a kind of schematic outline of the structure) is expressed by the term *tonu,* a Dogon word that means "portray." This relates to the Egyptian word *tennu,* which means "border or boundary."[4] The fourth and final stage of the metaphor is defined by the Dogon word *toymu,* which means "complete." The term relates to the Egyptian word *temau,* which also means "complete."[5]

Like the daily symbolic acts of Dogon life, these metaphoric progressions were tied symbolically to plants, animals, and actions that were common to everyday Dogon village life, and so took on a mnemonic aspect. The average Dogon tribe member would step out of his or her hut into a world that served to continually reinforce the tribe's cosmological teachings. When we consider the persistent effect of these various reinforcing cues to memory, it becomes understandable how Dogon society could have retained its form and the coherency of its cosmological tradition over a period of several thousand years.

2

Symbolic Constructs of the Cosmology

Many would say that the defining statement of ancient cosmology is expressed by the words "as above, so below," a phrase that is often interpreted to imply that the processes of the macrocosmic universe are in some way fundamentally similar to the microcosmic processes that create matter. Simple observation suggests that the two are similar; even a middle-school science student can see obvious similarities between an electron that orbits the nucleus of an atom and a planet that revolves around a star. Many of the symbolic themes of the various traditions we are studying can be seen as metaphors for this same defining phrase. For example, the earliest creator-deities of ancient China are pictured holding tools of measurement in their hands; the mother goddess Nu-wa holds a compass, which she uses to measure the circularity of the heavens, and the creator-god Fu-xi holds a carpenter's square, with which to measure the squareness of the Earth. These ancient Chinese images imply that a fundamental relationship exists between the macrocosm and the microcosm, which calls out for reconciliation. Within that same mindset, symbolic constructs of the cosmology are often given from each of these two perspectives: one that is macrocosmic, and another that is microcosmic.

Mythic definitions that relate to the macrocosm begin with a cosmogonic egg that is described as containing all of the future "seeds" of the universe. In reference to their creator-god Amma, the Dogon refer to this structure as Amma's egg. The Dogon priests say that this egg was the product of two inward-facing "thorns," likely correlates to two black holes in the terminology of modern astrophysics. For astronomers, a black hole is a point in space-time, such as a collapsed star, that has become so very massive that it draws in virtually everything that comes within its field of gravitational pull. The Dogon say that for a long period of time, these two "thorns" were able to hold the primordial matter they contained in stasis, but that this matter began to spin ever more quickly until a point was reached when it simply could no longer be contained. At that stage, the egg ruptured, scattering "pellets of clay"—correlates to astronomical bodies—to all corners of the universe. Using images that seem intentionally symbolic, the Dogon myth of the creation of the universe (see page 15) compares the sun to a clay pot that has been raised to a high heat and the moon to dry, dead clay.

Dogon descriptions of matter in its microcosmic wavelike state also begin with an egg, one that is conceptualized as the heart of a symbolic fish called the nummo fish. Like the Dogon and Egyptian

Figure 2.1. Dogon thorns held in stasis
(from Scranton, *Cosmological Origins*, 98)

terms *bummo* and *bu maa,* this Dogon word *nummo* also can be compared to an Egyptian term, *nu maa.* The Dogon, like modern astrophysicists, believe that matter begins as waves and is transformed by an act of perception into particles. The Dogon/Egyptian term *nu* refers to waves or water, and the term *ma* or *maa* implies the concept "to examine" or "perceive." The Dogon priests create a drawing of the nummo fish that serves as a diagram to illustrate the kinds of transformations that are said to occur just after matter in its wavelike state has been perceived.

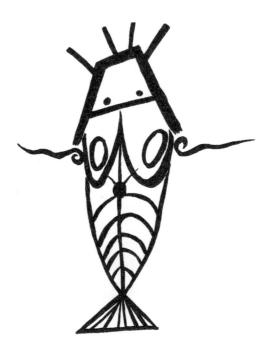

Figure 2.2. Dogon nummo fish drawing
(from Scranton, *Cosmological Origins,* 112)

From this perspective on creation, the egg, which is located where we would expect the heart of the fish to be, represents the point of perception of a wave. The notion of matter in its wavelike state is conveyed by the lines that define the tail of the fish. The collarbones (the Dogon say "clavicles") of the fish depict the wave as it draws up in response to this act of perception, creating a shape that the Dogon compare to a tent cloth that has been pulled upward from the center. From there, the waves on either side of the peak of this "tent" begin to vibrate and encircle, creating a series of primordial "bubbles." The first six of these "bubbles" ultimately collapse under their own weight, then after the seventh cycle they produce a sustainable bundle that the Dogon describe as the egg of the world. The Dogon conceive of this bundle as seven rays of a star of increasing length and characterize it by the spiral shape that can be drawn to inscribe the endpoints of the rays. This egg is a conceptual counterpart to the Calabi-Yau space in string theory, which is conceived of similarly as a bundle of collapsed dimensions that is said to exist at every point in space-time.

Inherent in these definitions, from the point just after the perceived wave rises up, are the cosmological concepts of duality and of the pairing of opposites. In fact, the Dogon priests define these two attributes as fundamental principles of the universe. As a reflection of these principles, many of the symbolic definitions of the cosmology are given in opposing pairs, through concepts that can be expressed symbolically in numerous ways. In some cases these principles are reflected in the pairing of male and female deities. In other cases, such as the Chinese concept of yin and yang, they are depicted as complementary shapes defined in opposing colors (traditionally black and white in the case of the yin/yang symbol). When describing the primordial elements of water, fire, wind, and earth, these principles are expressed as opposing aspects of each element.

There is also little question but that the concept of the aligned ritual shrine stands as the foremost symbolic construct of the creation tradition. Both the Dogon and the Buddhists assert this to be true, and each treats these structures as a kind of grand mnemonic symbol for the entire tradition. Stupa shrines are readily found all across India and Asia, and comparable structures take many variant forms in other widespread regions of the world. These forms begin with the simplest stone cairn and end with the Great Pyramid of Giza. A host of shared symbolic attributes argue that this class of aligned shrine includes such diverse types as the Mongolian yurt, Navajo roundhouse, Native American tepee, and even the traditional Jewish huppah. Again, for the sake of convenient terminology within this study, our choice will be to refer to these structures under the heading of stupas or aligned ritual shrines.

So pivotal is the symbolism of the stupa to the cosmological tradition that, by strictest interpretation, the shrine is assigned the role of a purely symbolic structure, one that is actually prohibited in some cultures from being put to any practical use. In fact, the dimensions that are given by the Dogon priests as measurements for their aligned granary include an internal contradiction in math, such that the shrine simply cannot be built precisely as defined. Everyday Dogon agricultural granaries that are actually used to store grain bear only a modest resemblance to the symbolic structure that is outlined in their cosmological tradition.

As the Dogon explain it, alignment of the ritual shrine was one of the first instructed exercises presented by their ancestor-teachers, but specific details about how the shrine was to be aligned are perhaps best explained in the Buddhist tradition. The practical requirements for accomplishing this alignment make good sense, when looked at from the perspective of a group of knowledgeable teachers faced with the task of implementing them in an environment where basic tools and materials for construction might not have been readily available. Alignment of the base plan of the stupa begins as a rudimentary exercise in geometry, where the first task is simply to draw a circle around a defined center or point.

It is important to understand that the alignment method for a stupa rests on proportional relationships that hold true for geometric figures of any size and so did not require a standardized unit of measure or a refined set of tools for precisely measuring them. Appropriate to that requirement, the ancient teachers apparently established the concept of a cubit, a unit of measure that could be marked out in relation to a person's own body. Like other concepts that are put forth in our cosmological plan, the cubit was assigned two distinct definitions: By one definition, the cubit represented the distance from a person's elbow to the tip of the middle finger. By another, it represented the average step or pace of a person as he or she walked.

As support for the view that the cubit was seen as a relative unit of measure as opposed to a precise one, we cite A. E. Berriman's classic book *Historical Metrology: A New Analysis of the Archaeological and the Historical Evidence Relating to Weights and Measures,* where Berriman provides a long list of ancient cultures known to have used cubits, alongside the many variant unit lengths that were applied to the measure.[1] Likewise, we know that within a given culture such as ancient Egypt, different cubit lengths seem to have coexisted, perhaps defined for different purposes or in relation to different symbolic concepts. One should also keep in mind that each two-dimensional geometric figure that appears within the cosmology was also likely to have a three-dimensional correlate. This means, for example, that any symbolism that is assigned to a circle would also apply similarly to a sphere.

The center of the circular base plan of the stupa was defined by a stick that was placed vertically in the ground. In some cultures, an additional step was taken that involved using a plumb line to assure that the stick was actually set vertically. Next, a simple line of radius was marked out from the stick, measured at twice the length of the stick itself, and a circle was then drawn around it. Using the shadows cast by the stick (or gnomon) in the sun, this base plan of the aligned stupa shrine served as a functional sundial by which an initiate could effectively track the hours of a day. The need for accurate timekeeping constituted one of the prerequisites for a working system of agriculture.

As the next step in aligning the shrine, the initiate marked the two longest of the stick's shadows of the day (one in the morning and one in the evening) at the points where they crossed the circle. These two points were then connected with a line that, because the sun rises in the east and sets in the west, automatically took on an east-west orientation and so defined an east-west axis for the circle. With the geometry of this added line, the sundial now became a tool capable of tracking the apparent motions of the sun throughout the year, and so gave visibility both to the concepts of a season and a year. Furthermore, if an initiate were to plot the east-west line every day with regularity, he or she would see that it passed through the stick on only two days of the year, on the dates of the two equinoxes. After that, the line would move progressively farther away from the stick until the next solstice, at which point the line would reverse its direction of motion.

In the next stage of the alignment of the shrine, the initiate drew two additional circles of a slightly larger radius than the first, each centered on one of the two endpoints of the east-west line. The larger radius caused these circles to overlap one another, intersecting at two new points. These points defined a second line that was perpendicular to the first, which served as a north-south axis for the circle. Taken together, the two intersecting axes divided the original circle (the circular base plan of the shrine) into four equal quadrants. This base plan, founded on a figure that the Dogon refer to as the egg in a ball, egg of the world, or the picture of Amma, would later be understood to be one of the central symbolic shapes of the cosmology.

At this point in the process, the alignment geometry of the ritual shrine was complete and produced matching ground plans for the Buddhist and Dogon shrines. However, in the next stage of the process, the circular base of the shrine would be effectively squared. The concept of reconciling two fundamental geometric figures, the circle and the square, is one that is central to ancient cosmology. From some perspectives the circle is symbolic of the creational processes of the universe or macrocosm, while the square relates symbolically to earth and to the microcosm where matter forms. Because of this, reconciling a circle with a square becomes a metaphor for the Hermetic phrase "As above, so below." In relation to the plan of the ritual shrine, this squaring was implemented in slightly different ways by the Dogon and the Buddhists. In the Dogon plan, the shrine rose ten cubits upward to a square, flat roof (leaving the shrine with a round base), while the Buddhists approach was to actually square the base of their stupa. Overt squaring of the circle in the Dogon system was accomplished by means of a second circle that was inscribed within the square of the roof. The Dogon priests assigned numeric measurements to their shrine that revealed an underlying rationale to their version of the plan: The central stick measured five cubits and the radius of the circle ten cubits, while the square roof of the Dogon granary was defined as eight cubits per side. Mathematically, if we apply 3.2 as an approximate value for pi, this produced a square whose numerical value of area matched the numerical value of the circumference of the circular base—both with a value of sixty-four—and so reflected a self-confirming measurement. Self-confirmation of measurements is an architectural feature that is indicative of deliberate design, and so suggests that the Dogon plan may preserve an original form.

Conceptually, the alignment of the base plan of the shrine was meant to define an ordered space (the Buddhists might say "sacred" or "ritualized" space) marked out from within the comparative disorder of an uncultivated field. In fact, in Dogon culture the act of cultivating land is conceptualized as bringing order to a disordered field. It is understood in both the Dogon and Buddhist traditions that this process of alignment replicates a primordial process of creation. Each component geometric figure evoked by the plan of the shrine carries symbolism that is shared commonly by the Dogon and the Buddhists, and there are multiple symbolic perspectives from which to view the shrine itself. The initial figure of the circle with its defined center is a product of the motions of the sun and is used to measure those motions, so it is understandable that it came to symbolize both the

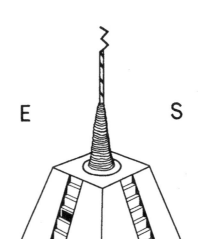

Figure 2.3. Dogon granary
(from Scranton, *Cosmological Origins*, 8)

sun and the concept of a day. For similar reasons, it is also easy to understand why the figure came to be associated with concepts relating to time measurement, such as a season or a year. Our contention based on how this same shape is applied in other symbolic contexts such as Egyptian hieroglyphic words is that it could also reasonably represent the motions of the Earth in relation to the sun, such as the daily rotation of the Earth on its axis and the annual revolution of the Earth around the sun.

For the Dogon, the square, flat roof of the granary represents the concept of "space" as it relates to matter, and the same symbolism applies to the squared base of the Buddhist shrine in its original round configuration, which is seen as "ritualized space." In both traditions the body of the aligned shrine is equated with a hemisphere, a three-dimensional geometric figure that conceptually reconciles the rounded dome of a circle with the base of a square. For the Dogon this hemisphere signifies "mass or matter," while for the Buddhists it represents the very similar concepts of "essence" or "substance."

The two derived axes of the base plan of the shrine are understood to define the cardinal points and were specifically given in reference to the geographic directions of east, west, north, and south. As suggested on page 27, these axes can be alternately conceived of in three dimensions by imagining that the central stick or gnomon defines a third vertical axis. This three-dimensional figure, which consists of six rays and a seventh central point, mimics the seven rays of the Dogon egg of the world, the essential underlying structure of matter, and so from this perspective the shrine itself can be seen as a symbolic representation of this egg.

The two-dimensional divided circular figure that evolves as the base plan of the aligned ritual shrine is alternately referred to by the Dogon as the egg in a ball or the picture of Amma. According to the Dogon priests, the central point of the figure is actually conceived of as another very small circular space, which is where the Dogon creator-god Amma is found. Although this idea is not spoken of in public, Amma is considered to be so small as to be effectively "hidden" and is understood to be dual in nature (from one perspective, Amma is interpreted to be both male and female). To underscore these points, the plan for the Dogon granary shrine provides that a small cup holding two even smaller grains be placed at the center point of the shrine.

The two defined axes of the base plan of the shrine (one with an east-west orientation and the other aligned north-south) symbolize the *axis mundi,* the "axis of the world." The concept of the axis mundi is often alternately represented in myth as a world tree, whose significance is taken to apply both to microcosmic matter and to the macrocosmic universe. However, commonalities exist between Dogon and ancient Chinese mythic references that suggest that in the original plan of cosmology, two symbolic trees may have been conceptualized. The first is described as a mulberry tree that is rooted in the primordial waters and grows upward through the conceptual worlds of matter. The second mythical tree, whose associations may have been primarily to the biological-reproductive theme of creation, is commonly referred to as the tree of life and is sometimes interpreted to have been a palm tree. One ancient Egyptian term for this tree is *aama*,[2] a word that calls to mind the name of the Dogon creator-god, Amma. In the Dogon and Egyptian cultures, this dual-tree symbolism seems to have survived in the more generic form of a single world tree or tree of life.

From other perspectives, Adrian Snodgrass relates that the stupa symbolizes a cosmic mountain that stands at the center of the universe.[3] The mountain is an important symbolic concept in many of the cosmological traditions we are studying, one that pertains both to the creation tradition and to the civilizing plan. The spire on top of a traditional stupa symbolically represents a "hair tuft" or topknot of hair that stands at the summit of that symbolic mountain.

There is another perspective on the symbolism of the Dogon granary shrine that associates its structural elements with bodies of the solar system. In this view, the circular base represents the sun, the circle that is inscribed within the square of the roof represents the moon, and the shrine itself represents the Earth—the astronomical body that lies conceptually between the sun and the moon.

The plan of the aligned ritual shrine defines its symbolic elements in a way that might be confusing to some researchers and may have caused some to suspect that a reversal in symbolism had occurred at some point in the history of the tradition. Based on the discussion of the primordial Chinese deities in my book *China's Cosmological Prehistory,* a circle is symbolic of the heavens, which we associate with the modern term *space,* while a square is associated with *earth,* a term that we interpret symbolically to refer to "mass or matter." But in the plan of the ritual shrine it is the figure of the square that overtly represents space. To my way of thinking, this confusion arises from what may be fundamentally a linguistic problem, which was likely caused by modern-day changes in meanings for the word *space.* As we proceed, we will see that there are multiple perspectives from which to consider the geometric figures of the circle and the square, and so the symbolism may not always seem to have been entirely clear-cut or consistent.

Important alternate symbolism attaches to the plan of the aligned ritual shrine as it relates to the biological-reproductive theme of the cosmology. From this perspective, the shrine is associated with the expanding womb of a woman, and the center of its circular base plan is considered to represent a navel. From this point of view, the related axis is interpreted as an *omphalos munde* or *umbilicus mundi,* essentially the symbolic umbilical cord of the world.

In their context within the Dogon egg-in-a-ball figure, the four defined quadrants of the base plan of the aligned shrine are associated with the four classic elements of water, fire, wind, and earth, and so represent the four progressive stages in the creation of matter, as previously

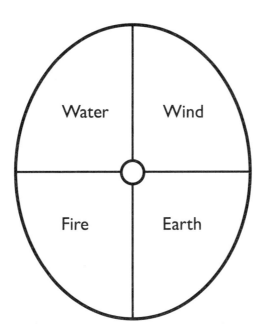

Figure 2.4. Dogon egg-in-a-ball drawing
(from Scranton, *Cosmological Origins,* 63)

discussed. This association underscores the symbolic relationship of the shrine to the components of matter.

These quadrants define the layout of the four lower compartments of the granary shrine, but the structure is constructed in three dimensions, and the plan also calls for four upper compartments, for a total of eight, symbolizing the eight cultivated grains of Dogon culture. From the standpoint of cosmology, these compartments also represent the eight component stages of the egg of the world, which include the seven collapsed dimensions of matter that initially comprise the egg and an eighth conceptual stage in which the bubble-like egg is ruptured. The rupturing of the egg is also said to initiate the formation of a new egg. Descriptions given by the Dogon priests suggest that these eggs combine together in a series to become counterparts to the membranes of matter that are defined in string theory.

Symbolic constructs of cosmology such as the ones we have been discussing are understood to have preceded written language in ancient cultures. However, as we will see, the suggestion is that they provided a set of ready-made conceptual images that could then be adapted to symbolic written language.

3

Constructs of the Language of Cosmology

Relationships between the cosmology and ancient languages begin with the Egyptian sun glyph, ☉, which takes the same essential form and symbolism as the base plan of the aligned ritual shrine. This glyph, associated with the same cosmological meanings as the shrine figure, is also found in the hieroglyphic language of the Tibetan Na-Khi tribe and in the earliest known system of Chinese writing, known as the oracle bone script. A squared version of the same shape, carrying the same symbolic meanings, seems to have passed forward into later Chinese hieroglyphic writing. In the case of ancient China, we can flatly rule out simple coincidence as a possible explanation for the similarity of the shapes because of the match that is presented by two correlating words, the Egyptian and Chinese hieroglyphic words for "week." Both are written with just two glyphs—the sun glyph and the number ten—and both reflect a correct symbolic definition of the ancient Chinese and Egyptian ten-day weeks. The match suggests that both written forms, along with matching calendar systems, derived from a single source, and this adds credence to the viewpoint that the source was a shared system of cosmology.

Correlations between Dogon and ancient Egyptian words offer us certain insights into how the words of the cosmological plan were apparently formulated. Before we begin comparing cosmological words, we should first note that the equivalencies we will draw between Dogon and Egyptian words do not rest on standard linguistic etymologies, but rather, the words relate to one another in the same way as any other properly correlated cosmological elements, whether they be deities, myths, or symbols. For our purposes, words are equated based on multiple matching attributes that can be shown to coincide for each pair of correlated words. We should also mention that what are given in the Dogon tradition as multiple meanings of a single spoken word (since the Dogon have no written language) were often expressed as multiple homonyms in the Egyptian hieroglyphic language. This difference occurs because each discrete word meaning has its own unique spelling in relation to Egyptian glyphs, expressed through a variety of glyphs that carry similar pronunciations to one another.

For me, one of the most helpful aspects of the Dogon creation tradition is that each cosmological term carries at least two distinct definitions. These definitions are distanced from one another logically, so that knowing one of the definitions will not reasonably allow a person to guess the secondary meanings. For example, the term for the Dogon atom-like component of matter, *po,* can also refer to "the beginning of time." The likely Egyptian counterpart, *pau* or *pau-t,* refers to the concepts of "mass, matter, or substance," but is also pronounced like an Egyptian homonym that means "primordial time."

Furthermore, these meanings are tagged to the cosmological concepts they represent, not to a specific pronunciation in any given culture, and so the related meanings tend to hold their form across the boundaries of culture and language. So in the case of ancient Egypt or ancient China, where cosmological terms seem to have been pronounced similarly to those of the Dogon, we often find a three-way correlation among the Chinese, Dogon, and Egyptian pronunciations that is also founded on at least two shared meanings for the word. In the case of the Vedic or Buddhist traditions, where words are given in a language that is outwardly quite different from the Dogon language, we find that cosmological concepts are still associated with the same predictive set of meanings that apply to their Dogon, Egyptian, and Chinese counterparts. In many cases, a word may also relate to comparable mythological characters or deities who share similar attributes, are credited with performing the same mythic acts, are credited with the introduction of specific and similar civilizing skills, or are associated with matching icons. These diverse points of commonality create a unique "bundle" of criteria that is more than sufficient to validate any given correlation.

It became clear during our studies of Dogon and Egyptian cosmological words in *Sacred Symbols of the Dogon* that many cosmological words were formed by linking together predefined phonemes—root pronunciations that were already symbolic of specific concepts. From that perspective, it wouldn't matter whether you chose to pronounce a spoken word or spell a written word using glyphs of the same pronunciation, the implied cosmological concept would be the same. It appeared that if we could simply establish which concept to properly associate with each of the various phonemes, we could predict the meanings of cosmological words based on their pronunciation alone.

So I came to see that the term *na,* which defines the Dogon word for "mother," implied the same meaning of "mother" in the language of the Tibetan Na-Khi. Likewise we could see that the Dogon and Egyptian word *nu* implied the concept of primordial waves or water and that the Egyptian deity Nu was traditionally understood to be a goddess of the primeval waters. Relationships like these led us to understand that the name of the Dogon creator-god, Amma, combines the phoneme *am,* meaning "knowledge" and implying the biblical connotation of "procreation," with the phoneme *ma,* meaning "to examine" or "perceive." These two meanings can be seen to represent the initiating acts of biological and cosmological creation, respectively.

From a broader perspective, in *Sacred Symbols of the Dogon* we defined a complex set of relationships between cosmological words and concepts in ancient Egypt that links:

A phonetic value,

The name of an Egyptian deity based on that same phonetic value,

The traditional mythological role assigned to that deity,

A defined cosmological stage of the creation of matter, and

An Egyptian glyph that carries the same phonetic value.

For example, the Dogon term *ke* refers both to "the creative force" and to a class of water beetles, including the dung beetle. We also know based on Dogon cosmological metaphors that insects were meant to symbolize processes that initiate creation. Budge assigns the Egyptian phonetic value *khep* to the beetle glyph and the name Kheper to a beetle-headed creator-deity.[1] Based on these references, we could place the Egyptian deity Kheper and the Egyptian beetle glyph at the beginning stages of matter. (In Egyptian cosmology, the beetle represents the concept of nonexistence coming into existence.) From there, similar commonalities allowed us to define an extensive table of the progressive stages of matter, expressed entirely in terms of these same elements: ancient phonetic values, Dogon and Egyptian cosmological words, Egyptian deities, and Egyptian glyphs.

As our studies revealed likely symbolic meanings for more and more Egyptian glyph shapes, we found that many Egyptian hieroglyphic words could be interpreted symbolically, in much the same way as we just discussed in regard to the Egyptian word for "week." We found that if we simply substituted the proper concept for each glyph in a written Egyptian word, we could produce a symbolic sentence whose meaning effectively defined the word. As an example, the glyphs of one Egyptian word for "month" can reasonably be read to mean "the moon makes an orbit."[2]

Furthermore, we noticed that the spelling of certain Egyptian words includes a trailing glyph that is not pronounced. Because the image conveyed by the glyph typically bears some relationship to the overall meaning of the word, many Egyptologists believe that these glyphs were attached to the words for emphasis. However, when we approached these words from a symbolic standpoint rather than phonetically, it became apparent that the interpreted reading of the word was meant to define a meaning for the trailing glyph. In other words, an apparent mechanism existed by which the Egyptian hieroglyphic language effectively defined the symbolic meanings of its own glyphs. This realization made it possible to develop a long list of Egyptian glyphs and associated symbolic meanings that, based on their spelling, could now be attributed to the Egyptian priests themselves.

Although the Dogon and Egyptian phonetic values were of little use to us in any comparison to Sanskrit words of the ancient Buddhist tradition, we found that the phonetic sentences that seemed to define each Egyptian word effectively transformed Budge's *An Egyptian Hieroglyphic Dictionary* into a cosmological encyclopedia, where the form of each word held potential information regarding the intended meanings of various cosmological concepts. Furthermore, Genevieve Calame-Griaule's *Dictionnaire Dogon* is structured in such a way that it often provides expanded definitions for words whose meanings relate to cosmology through the commentary and insights that Calame-Griaule provides. Also, the Dogon words tend to take a very simple form, one that often coincides with the root phonetic values on which various cosmological terms seem to be based. Other Dogon words consist of fairly obvious compounds of these root terms, and so uphold our outlook on how terms of ancient cosmology may have been formulated.

One very helpful insight based on the commonality of ancient phonemes centers on the name of the Dogon fifty-year festival of Sirius, called the Sigi. This term is a likely correlate to the Egyptian word *skhai,* which means "to celebrate a festival." The collective name given to the predynastic Amazigh tribes can be seen to combine the name of the creator-god Amma with the Egyptian word *skhai* to produce the compound *amma-skhai,* or *amazigh,* which conveys the meaning "celebrates Amma." Likewise, the name of the Tibetan Na-Khi (or Na-Xi) tribe can be interpreted to combine Na (a name for the mother goddess) with the same Egyptian term *skhai* for a combined meaning of "celebrates Na." Due to the sparseness of evidence, Chinese scholars cannot be certain whether the name Fu-xi (sometimes given as Pau-xi), the ostensible name of the Chinese creator-god, actually referred to a deity, an emperor, a dynasty of rulers, or a tribe. Based purely on the form of the word itself, which also combines the cosmologically significant root phonemes Fu or Pau with the suffix "xi," this apparent naming convention suggests that the term was a tribal name.

It was also extremely helpful that many of the Chinese cosmological words were given in terms of familiar Dogon and Egyptian phonemes, an eventuality that opened a door to the unlikely use of the Dogon and Egyptian dictionaries as productive resources for interpreting ancient Chinese terms. Like other traditions we are studying, Chinese cosmological words were given in relation to paired definitions, and as with our Dogon studies, these definitions made correlation to the Dogon and Egyptian dictionaries both possible and credible. The net result of our language comparisons was to provide us with a working set of resources with which to test the likely meanings of various concepts and terms of the cosmology. To the extent that we find these resources to be in agreement about the meaning of a given term, we can be confident about any interpretation we put forward for that term. Each time the glyphs of an Egyptian word affirm that interpretation, we gain a higher degree of confidence about our understanding of the meanings of those symbols.

4

Gobekli Tepe and Zep Tepi

Gobekli Tepe is a megalithic site from the Neolithic era located in southeastern Turkey that, based on artifacts uncovered there, appears to have been in use some eleven thousand years ago. Based on traditional historical timelines, the site actually predates the earliest evidence we have of the tools that should have been required to build it. It consists of a man-made mound or *tell* that housed a megalithic sanctuary with numerous round enclosures consisting of stone pillars connected by walls built from smaller stone blocks, along with stone benches. Some researchers surmise that at the time of their construction, the stone pillars may have been used to support a roof; in fact, one of the meanings of the Turkish word *tepe* actually is "roof." However, because any such roof is likely to have been constructed from materials that would have been less durable than stone, evidence of it simply may not have survived.

Finely worked images of animals and birds, serpents and scorpions, some presented in high relief and often still quite well preserved, were carved into many of the massive stone pillars at the site. These were sometimes also decorated in low relief with stylized arms and hands, belts and loincloths, suggesting to researchers that they may have symbolized ancestors. Prominent carved images of vultures give the impression that the sanctuary may have been the site of ritual "sky burials" that are known to have been practiced in early times by ancient cultures such as the Tibetans. Such cultures often placed the body of a dead person on a high mountaintop to be scavenged by birds of prey. Several large carved sculptures uncovered at the site reflect similarities to North American totem poles.

Indications are that the site was carefully and deliberately buried sometime within approximately a thousand years of its construction. This circumstance protected the site from weathering over the following millennia and so is largely credited for the remarkable state of its preservation. Based on our current state of knowledge, the people who inhabited the region where Gobekli Tepe is situated would have still been living as hunter-gatherers at the time of its construction, since no known civic centers existed at the time. No significant evidence has been uncovered to indicate that people ever actually inhabited this site—no fire pits or trash heaps have been unearthed, and there is no nearby water source—nor has more than incidental evidence of tools of the type that must have been used in the site's construction been recovered. So far in the excavations, few human bones have been discovered at the site. To our knowledge, the structures at Gobekli Tepe predate any formal human settlement anywhere. If, in fact, these megalithic pillars functioned in ancient times as a temple, then it would be fair to say that the site constituted the very first known temple.[1]

For anyone who is familiar with the origin myths of ancient Egypt, the discovery of a primordially ancient site such as this one in Turkey, linked to the term *tepe,* can only call to mind familiar Egyptian references to a mythical First Time, which is referred to by the term Zep Tepi or by variations or transpositions of that term. In his Egyptian dictionary Budge lists the word as *sep tepi* and defines it to mean "primeval time" or "lands of primeval time."[2] The term is based on a phonetic root that essentially means "time, occasion, or circumstance" and is written with glyphs that, based on our understanding of cosmological symbolism, read "the binding of space and time." This concept is given in terms of the square glyph and the circular Egyptian time glyph, and so might possibly be seen as symbolic of the act of reconciling a square with a circle. In our view, the concept of squaring a circle can also be taken as a metaphor for the phrase "as above, so below."

Figure 4.1. Egyptian word *sep,*
which means "primeval time" or "lands of primeval time"
(see Budge, *Egyptian Hieroglyphic Dictionary,* 596a)

Budge gives several hieroglyphic spellings for the word *sep,* including one that, from our perspective, defines the same flying goose glyph, , that symbolizes the concept of matter in the correlated Dogon and Egyptian words *po* and *pau-t.* This term can also mean "primeval time" for the Egyptians and "the beginning of time" for the Dogon. Another of Budge's spellings defines the fox glyph, , which in relation to the concept of time Budge pronounces *sep.* The fox is an animal that stands as a defining symbol for the entire Dogon cosmological tradition. In fact, the title of Griaule and Dieterlen's definitive study of the Dogon religion is *The Pale Fox.* Both the goose and the fox are animals that are pictured in carvings at Gobekli Tepe. Another of Budge's word entries for *sep,* which is given in terms of the same leading glyphs, means "worm" or "serpent," and defines the serpent glyph, , another animal that is pictured at Gobekli Tepe.

R. T. Rundle Clark writes in *Myth and Symbol in Ancient Egypt* in regard to this very ancient Egyptian tradition of the First Time, "The basic principles of life, nature and society were determined by the gods long ago, before the establishment of the kingship. This epoch—'Tep Zepi'–'the First Time'—stretched from the first stirring of the High God in the Primeval Waters to the settling of Horus upon the throne and the redemption of Osiris. All proper myths relate events or manifestations of this epoch. . . . Anything whose existence or authority had to be justified or explained must be referred to the 'First Time' . . . which was a golden age of absolute perfection."[3]

In our studies of the cosmological traditions of ancient China, we found that ancient language, even in the absence of surviving written texts, could be an effective tool for interpreting the meanings of important concepts and symbols. These interpretations became possible largely because of the ever-higher degree of commonality we find among ancient cosmological terms as the references move further backward in time. So our first impulse when attempting to understand the range of symbolic elements presented at Gobekli Tepe was to look to various languages for help.

Realizing that cosmologically significant words tend to hold their meanings over long periods of time within the context of a culture's language, our first step was to examine modern-day meanings for the Turkish word *tepe*. What we found (using Turkish language dictionaries) was upward of twenty-five distinct meanings that could be alternately assigned to the word. Then, as a practical test of our observation about commonality of ancient language, we turned to Budge's *An Egyptian Hieroglyphic Dictionary* and discovered that we were able to correlate at least a dozen of those meanings to Egyptian words whose pronunciations were based on the phonetic root *tep*. In essence, these comparisons demonstrated that when the ancient Egyptians used the words *tep* or *tepe*, they likely understood the meaning in the same essential ways as someone in ancient Turkey.

Furthermore, several of these Egyptian meanings have apparent significance in terms of Gobekli Tepe itself. For example, according to Budge the Egyptian word *tepi a* means "ancestor" or "predecessor,"[4] which is what the anthropomorphized pillars at Gobekli Tepe are surmised to represent. The Turkish word *tepe* can refer to a hill, a peak, a mountain, or a summit (all terms that physically describe Gobekli Tepe), and Budge defines an Egyptian word, *tep*, to mean "high ground" or "the top of anything."[5]

The translated meaning that is most often given for Gobekli Tepe is "potbelly hill." However, alternate meanings for the words suggest other reasonable interpretations, many of which reflect possible relationships to our plan of cosmology. For example, the Turkish word *gobek* means "midpoint," "navel," or "umbilicus," which supports an interpretation of the term Gobekli Tepe that means "hill with a navel," reflecting symbolism that characterizes a Buddhist stupa. The Turkish word *tepe* can also mean "topknot" or "summit," two terms that could also associate the name with symbolic themes of a stupa.

There are also phonetic relationships between the term *sep* and important Egyptian deities who have significance for our cosmology. For instance, Budge refers to Sep as a Heliopolitan form of Osiris, an Egyptian god who is closely linked with civilizing skills and is sometimes associated with the constellation of Orion.[6] Septit is an Egyptian name for the Dog Star, also known as Sothis or Sirius.[7]

Next we approached the carved images at Gobekli Tepe from a cosmological perspective. From the outset, we could see that certain carvings on the Gobekli Tepe megaliths depict animals that play symbolic roles in the cosmologies we study. For instance, there are images of serpents, which by our interpretation represent the concept of the first completed "Word," or underlying structure of matter, and as we have said there is an image of a fox, which is symbolic of the Dogon cosmology itself. There are representations of geese, which figure largely in one of the four-stage symbolic metaphors of the cosmology. However, there are also animals portrayed in these carvings that, based on our experience with the Dogon, Egyptian, and Buddhist traditions, played no obvious cosmological role at all. So, if we began with the premise that the Gobekli Tepe images were meant to be cosmological in nature, how were we to interpret these seemingly noncosmological animals?

In search of clues to this mystery, we looked to word entries in Budge's dictionary that define the names of these animals. I discovered that each animal pictured at Gobekli Tepe—both those with and without known cosmological symbolism—was assigned an Egyptian name that was pronounced like a Dogon/Egyptian term of cosmology. I had arrived at this insight prior to writing the previous book of this series, *China's Cosmological Prehistory,* and it proved to be quite helpful when exploring the possible symbolism of various animals that are pictured in the ancient Chinese zodiac. Conversely, the ancient Chinese references also suggested that in archaic times, progressive stages of creation had been associated symbolically and linguistically with various creatures of the animal kingdom.

This apparent association between specific animals and stages of creation cast the images at Gobekli Tepe in a new light. Knowing that the site itself is thought to have long predated actual written language, it occurred to me that these images might have constituted a kind of protowriting, whereby a hunter-gatherer, who would have been quite familiar with the names of these local animals, would see an image, say the animal's name aloud, and by so doing also speak a term of cosmology. From that perspective, Gobekli Tepe might well have been built as an instructional center, one of the remote places where mythical ancestors of our ancient tradition were ostensibly taken for their initial civilizing instruction.

The Gobekli Tepe site is in a region of the Fertile Crescent that is located nearby where the earliest documented evidence of domesticated wheat, animal husbandry, and metallurgy are found. These are three specific skills that are consistently associated with the civilizing plan by the various cultures we are studying. To have also found the earliest example of advanced stone masonry and megalithic construction (found at Gobekli Tepe itself) located in the same region and dated to the same approximate era certainly suggested that some major cultural transition may have occurred here.

When we approach the mysteries of Gobekli Tepe from this point of view, that the site's primary purpose might possibly have been to serve as an instructional center, then several of the more confusing aspects of its mystery seem to resolve. If ancient humanity had outside help in our move upward toward civilization (as many of the ancient cultures claim) then it makes sense that we might not see an archeological progression of tool development there before we see actual carved megaliths. Next, refined stone masonry is one of the hallmarks of the ancient cultures we are studying. Here we find its seemingly abrupt appearance in a setting that could well suggest instruction in the same context that many ancient traditions actually describe: a high mountaintop sanctuary. It also seems significant that what has been preserved at Gobekli Tepe are examples of stonework as a refined skill, not the fledgling beginnings of what might eventually grow into a refined stonework tradition. The placement of the pillars at Gobekli Tepe would also have required great practiced skill when it came to the extraction and transportation of mammoth slabs of stone. Clearly, some people on the scene at that time knew precisely what they were doing when it came to stone quarrying and masonry and were in possession of appropriate tools to accomplish those tasks.

The many outwardly similar circles of stone pillars found at Gobekli Tepe might seem somewhat confusing when we interpret them as having been placed there simply as a temple. Based on their stratigraphy, they were built over an extended period of time, but while the earlier structures were obviously still standing and in good repair (as they largely still are now), so the motivation for building so many seemingly redundant structures seems somewhat murky. But matching structures make pretty good sense if we surmise that each might have been constructed as the final project of its own graduating class of ancestor-initiates whose education at Gobekli Tepe included training in the skills of stonemasonry. Likewise, the puzzling similarities of style that are often observed to exist in ancient stonework from widespread regions of the world (often located in high mountain settings comparable to Gobekli Tepe) might also make sense if we imagine them to have been the work of graduated initiates who all learned their skills from a single common group of ancient instructors.

We observed previously that the esoteric tradition of the Dogon functioned to block entry to insincere outsiders, and so reflected a perceived need to hide certain information, although from whom or for what purpose may not be entirely clear. On reflection, the deliberate burial of the Gobekli Tepe megaliths makes very little rational sense, especially given the immense amount of work that must have been required to construct them initially and the considerable additional work that would have been required later to fully bury them without also damaging the structures. Surely in that era, any culture capable of undertaking such projects would also have been more than capable of defending them against the arrows, spears, and wooden clubs of any menacing hunter-gatherers. Likewise, of all existing structures of that era, these immense megaliths should have seemed impregnable, capable of weathering most known natural threats. So if the likely motive for burying them was not to protect them, then why bother to bury them at all? It would make as much sense for the ancient Greeks to have buried the Parthenon.

The esoteric tradition itself, which we observed was designed to conceal information from insincere outsiders, suggests one possible answer to this question: to hide them (or perhaps to hide the instructional tradition they represented) from some as-yet-unnamed outside group. The Dogon priests say that after a period of time, their revered ancestor-teachers were forced to leave and that this event was seen as a turning point in the history of humanity. Other ancient cultures we have studied maintain similar beliefs, that after a time their revered ancestor-teachers or ancestor-gods either chose to leave or were forced to leave. If Gobekli Tepe had been an instructional site and the parties involved knew with certainty that further instruction would no longer be conducted there, then nothing of value would have been lost by burying the site. Whatever the true motive may have been for burying these Neolithic megaliths, we can presume that it must have been a truly exceptional one: just imagine a group of 1950s Catholics deliberately choosing to physically bury the cathedral in which they had long worshipped. Another possible answer to the question is that whoever built the site wanted to preserve it for posterity, and they knew that burying it would accomplish that. In this case, covering over the site after its instructional purposes had been fulfilled might possibly have been part of the original plan.

Aspects of many of the symbolic elements that are exhibited at Gobekli Tepe are expressed by Egyptian words that center on the phonetic root *tem*. These include a series of words that are actually pronounced *tem,* one of which Budge defines to mean "enclosure."[8] Two other *tem* words mean "to cut, to engrave, to inscribe"[9] and "to cut an inscription."[10] *Tem* is an Egyptian word for "scorpion," a creature whose carved image is found at Gobekli Tepe. It also means "to be stung or bitten by a reptile."[11] Another of Budge's dictionary entries is for the word *temiu,* meaning "full (dual of the two hands),"[12] and so could relate to the two carved arms and hands we see on a Gobekli Tepe pillar. Likewise there is an Egyptian word *tem* that means "to praise," and so relates to Gobekli Tepe in its possible role as a temple.[13]

Through several additional meanings, the Egyptian word *tem* also links us to the notion of instructed initiation in the Dogon sense. These begin with definitions that relate directly to the concept of an initiate. Budge tells us that the word *tem* can also mean "to finish, complete, come to an end" and "to shut the mouth."[14] We know from our Dogon studies that these define the two obligations in the Dogon esoteric tradition of initiates, who were charged with "completing the words" of the cosmology and "remaining silent" about the secrets of that cosmology when in the presence of noninitiates.

Concepts of ritual burial that have been suggested for the Gobekli Tepe site are reflected in a word *tem* that means "to die or perish"[15] and by the word *tema,* defined by Budge as "to be united with the earth" or "dead."[16] Yet another Egyptian word, *tems,* means "to hide, to cover over," and so seems to predict the eventual fate of the Gobekli Tepe site itself.[17]

If the creation tradition that we have been exploring had its roots at Gobekli Tepe, then we would expect to find essential elements of that tradition in ancient Turkic cosmology, and in actual fact, we do. As is true for the Dogon, in ancient Turkey matter was conceived of as existing in three worlds that were associated symbolically with a world tree, which also served as a conceptual axis for the universe. Images of Turkic shamans traditionally show them holding a round drum whose hollow backside is supported by a pair of wooden slats that divide the circular drum into four quarters. This configuration repeats the Dogon figure of the egg in a ball, which was understood to be a conceptual starting point for creation. Likewise, the Dogon priests attribute the formation of matter to vibrations, a notion that is conveyed symbolically through the use of drums.

Because vultures are pictured prominently in carvings at Gobekli Tepe and figure largely in the sky burial rituals that are surmised to have been performed there, I began to explore what Dogon, Buddhist, and Egyptian sources have to say about vultures. The vulture is an ancient symbol for Sirius, and in Egypt two vultures together symbolize the Egyptian goddess Isis and her dark sister Nephthys. Budge defines the term *mu-t,* written with a single vulture glyph, 🦅, to mean "mother," and he calls Isis and Nephthys "the two Vulture mothers" or "ancestresses," and they are referred to as *mu-ti,* a word that is written with two vulture glyphs, 🦅 🦅.[18] Budge defines Mut as the Neith-like "Mother" goddess of all Egypt.[19] Calame-Griaule understands the Dogon word *mu* as a term of feminine relationship, and so the word could also apply to a mother.[20]

These same two goddesses were also referred to in Egypt as "vulture goddesses" under the term *ner-ti.*[21] My outlook is that traditional symbolic associations that exist between Isis and the bright star of Sirius (designated Sirius A by modern astronomers) strongly suggest that Nephthys represents the dark dwarf star (Sirius B) that accompanies it in the Sirius system. Unexpected Dogon knowledge of this difficult-to-see second star and the correct orbital period for the two stars is what first brought the Dogon into public controversy in 1975, with the publication of Robert Temple's book *The Sirius Mystery.* Another term Budge lists for "vulture" is *shta-t,* a phonetic pronunciation that also means "sanctuary or shrine" and "sarcophagus, grave, tomb or cemetery."[22] Yet a third term, *tcher or tcher-ti,* is applied to Isis and Nephthys as the "ancestresses"; Isis is the "Great Ancestress" and Nephthys the "Little Ancestress," designations that fit well with an interpretation of the goddesses as the larger and dwarf Sirius stars.[23] Budge tells us that these goddesses were alternately represented as women, as cows, and as birds. The *tchertiu* were "ancestors, forbears, predecessors, beings, human or divine, of ancient time." He also defines a term, *tcheri-t,* that refers to a shrine.

In our understanding of animal symbolism as it is applied in the creation tradition, symbolic meaning most often centers on some salient feature of the animal involved. One obvious attribute of a vulture is its ability to grasp things with its talons, and the notion of grasping is one that is assigned to the creator-gods Amma and Amen in the Dogon and Egyptian traditions. A symbolic reading of the glyphs of the Egyptian word *Amen*, which means "to grasp," shows that it relates to the concept of knowing, in very much the same sense that the modern word *grasp* means "to come to know." Of course, in the civilizing plan, knowledge is also explicitly associated with ancestors. From these perspectives, the notion of vultures in a symbolic relationship with ancestor goddesses and Sirius reaffirms the Dogon outlook that associates their ancestor-teachers with Sirius.

Calame-Griaule defines the Dogon concept of "vulture" as *tebe,* a word that can hardly fail to suggest the Turkish word *tepe*. There are two additional comments made in her dictionary entry that are of particular interest to us. First, she defines a vulture as being a "large-breasted eagle." Although the implied meanings are quite different, this statement coincides with a comment Budge makes in relation to the ner-ti vulture goddesses. Almost as an aside, he defines these goddesses as having "long abundant hair and pendent breasts."[24] One can easily imagine that, in the original tradition, vultures were compared with larger-breasted eagles, but that over time in Egypt, the bird association got lost in translation and transferred from the vultures to the mother goddesses. One other very interesting point Calame-Griaule makes that would seem to bring us back around to the notion of Gobekli Tepe as an instructional center is that the Dogon word *tebe* forms the root of the word *tebelu,* which refers to a "moment when humanity was restored to culture."[25]

As with deities in many ancient cultures, the vulture also has associations with the Buddha in the stupa tradition. Adrian Snodgrass tells us that the Buddha from the late centuries BCE whom we typically associate with the Buddhist tradition affirmed that there had been Buddhas in every previous age. It was understood that the first transmission of knowledge to humanity happened in a much earlier era at a place called Vulture Peak with an earlier Buddha. Of course, the term *peak* is yet another of the two-dozen meanings that are associated with the Turkish word *tepe.*

5

Archaic Temple Names

Having successfully used comparisons of language to define a number of likely connections between Gobekli Tepe and the other traditions we study, our next linguistically based step was to consider ancient names for the region of Turkey where Gobekli Tepe is located. According to Budge, one Greek term for the region was Cappadocia. As an appendix to *An Egyptian Hieroglyphic Dictionary,* Budge attached an "Index of Geographical Names" that includes an entry for the generalized term Cappadocia. This entry points us to an ancient Egyptian name for the region that Budge pronounces *Getpetkai.*

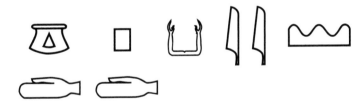

Figure 5.1. Egyptian word *Getpetkai* (ancient name for Cappadocia) (see Budge, *Egyptian Hieroglyphic Dictionary,* 1050a)

Allowing for the passage of nearly seven thousand years between the building of the sanctuary at Gobekli Tepe (around 10,000 BCE) and the earliest days of ancient Egypt (around 3000 BCE), the name Getpetkai would seem to offer a reasonable approximation for the modern word Gobekli. However, the glyphs used to write the earlier word present some interesting difficulties.

The first of these difficulties relates to the very first glyph in the word, a figure that Budge himself seems to be somewhat confused about: ⬜. This glyph takes the outward form of a flat-topped shrine, somewhat reminiscent of a stupa, but one that has been overlaid or inset with a conical shape. Budge assigns no descriptive significance to the glyph in his "List of Hieroglyphic Characters" at the front of his dictionary. He ultimately attributes a "g" sound to the glyph,[1] but compares it in the first of his dictionary entries with two Hebrew letters, *kuf* and *gimel*.[2] This suggests that he may not have settled on a definitive pronunciation for the glyph and implies that it could have reflected a complex "kg" sound, perhaps similar to the throaty Hebrew "ch" that is heard in the Hebrew name Chaim.

For my own convenience, and since Budge offers no opinion as to what the glyph symbolized, I initially referred to this figure as the fire altar glyph, in reference to the flame-shaped triangle it exhibited. In my efforts to come to an understanding of what the glyph represented, I presented several ideas to a knowledgeable acquaintance of mine, British archaeologist John Ward, including the possibility that it might represent the concept of a "fire altar." His outlook was that the figure could possibly represent a shrine with a viewing slot, of the type through which astronomical sightings of stellar risings and settings were made. I pursued his suggestion and found support for his outlook in the Egyptian word *teg,* meaning "to look at, to see," where the glyph appears to symbolize a structure that gives or facilitates sight.[3] The same glyph is evident in other Egyptian words that mean "to examine" or "to scrutinize," and so given those confirming examples, I now refer to it as the shrine glyph.

I could see that there must be some legitimacy to Budge's original pronunciation of the name, which he gives as *Getpetkai,* because a similar pronunciation had seemingly survived as the Turkish name Gobekli. However, further research into the term brought my attention to the Greek transliteration of the name of an ancient Egyptian temple in Memphis that was given similarly as Hwt-kA-ptH, or in Budge's terms,

Figure 5.2. Egyptian word *teg,* meaning "to look at, to see"
(see Budge, *Egyptian Hieroglyphic Dictionary,* 891a)

Het Ka Pet. This is the Greek term from which the name Egypt actually derives. The written form of this word, coupled with the complex phonetic value that Budge believes associates with our shrine glyph, supported *Het Pet Kai,* or "temple of Ptah and Ka," as an alternate pronunciation for the Egyptian name Getpetkai. Looked at in this way, the leading shrine glyph seemed to function like an Egyptian determinative and signal the name of a temple or sanctuary. However, in traditional Egyptian words, determinatives fall at the end of the word, not the beginning, so my supposition was that this might represent an archaic form.

As I explored other Egyptian words that made use of this same shrine glyph, I came across a second word, Ga nu sa Ast, which began with the shrine glyph, took the same general form as Getpetkai, and according to Budge, was also the name of an ancient Egyptian sanctuary located in Panopolis. He tells us that the name means "cradle of the son of Isis," which implies that it was associated with a mythical deity associated with the stars of Sirius. As yet, I know of no archaic sanctuary contemporary with Gobekli Tepe with which to positively associate the word.

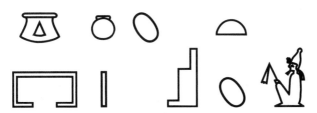

Figure 5.3. Egyptian word *Ga nu sa Ast*
(see Budge, *Egyptian Hieroglyphic Dictionary,* 800b)

However, unlike Het Pet Kai, which seems to make reference to only two deities, Pet and Ka, the name of this Panopolis temple, Ga nu sa Ast, was clearly defined in terms of the names of three deities. I initially took these to be Nu (goddess of the primeval waters), Sa (Osiris/Orion), and Ast (Isis/Sirius). If there is one thing I have learned over the course of two decades of study of this tradition, it is that whoever may have designed it seems to have been a stickler for consistency, and this outlook suggested that my interpretation of one of these two terms must be wrong. For me, the outward parallelism of the two words implied that each should be given in terms of the same number of deities.

After some reflection, it occurred to me that the double reed-leaf glyphs, 𓇌, that appear toward the end of Budge's name Getpetkai are likely correlates to the double yuds, ", in Hebrew that represent the name of the Hebrew god Yah. This meant that from a third perspective, the word could actually read Het Pet Ka Yah, meaning "temple of Ptah, Ka, and Yah," followed by the mountain glyph. Expressed in terms of the cosmological concepts we believe to be symbolized by these deities, this reading would make it a cosmological temple honoring space (Pet), duality (Ka), and light (Yah). This interpretation had the advantage of preserving what I perceived to be linguistic and symbolic parallels in the form of the two names: both names begin with the shrine glyph, signaling (based on what I perceived as an archaic convention) the name of a temple; both temple names were defined in terms of three deities; and both had well-known temple counterparts in ancient Egypt.

However, Budge's pronunciation of the second temple name was still formulated in terms of what I considered to be the archaic "ga" sound of the shrine glyph. My expectation based on the parallelism of the words was that I should also interpret a more modernized pronunciation for the name Ga nu sa Ast that would begin with the phonetic value *het,* comparable to Het Pet Ka Yah. Working from that approach, I surmised, based on Budge's more modernized view of the phonetic values of the glyphs, that the word could be pronounced alternately as *Het Penu Sa Ast.* The primary difficulty with this perspective was that

I was completely unaware of any deity in any of the cultures I study whose name was given as Penu. However, I also knew that the role of a good comparative cosmologist is to strive to follow wherever the symbolism seems to take you.

Looking again to Budge's dictionary, I discovered that *penu* was the Egyptian name for a mouse, that Budge also defines Penu as a "mythological mouse or rat," and that both words relate phonetically to an Egyptian god named Pen.[4] Budge also lists a word entry for a shrew mouse deity whose name was Hetes, whose name relates phonetically to my modernized pronunciation of the shrine glyph: *het.* Furthermore, I learned that an ancient shrew mouse god had actually been honored at two locations in ancient Egypt, both at Panopolis, where Budge's associated temple was located, and at Letopolis.

I could also see that the apparently archaic Turkish name Ga nu sa Ast is rooted in a term that might conceivably relate to the dancing elephant deity Ganesha, or Ganesa, in India; that, like the names Getpetkai and Gobekli, the root of the term Ga nu sa Ast might also have reasonably survived in India as Ganesha. And so I began to explore the archaic symbolism of Ganesha. Walter Fairservis says in *The Roots of Ancient India* that the worship of Ganesha grew out of roots that may be at least as old as the Harappan civilization, which is traditionally dated to the period around 3000 BCE.[5] Although the earliest surviving iconic images of Ganesha date from much later periods (at earliest, the late centuries BCE), Ganesha is traditionally pictured in the company of a rat or a mouse who somewhat comically serves as his vehicle of transport (or in Vedic terms, *vimana*).

Another possible translation of the term Gobekli Tepe comes from the Turkish word *gobek,* which can mean "midpoint" or "center." From that perspective, the term Gobekli Tepe translates as "central hill." If we look at a map of the region in eastern Turkey where Gobekli Tepe is located, we see that it is situated roughly equidistant from Africa, Egypt, India, Tibet, and China, and so the term might be appropriate to the kind of centrally sited ancient training center we imagine it to

have been. This same meaning of "central hill" also defines the suffix
–opolis in ancient Greece, where temples were traditionally built high
on a central hill and named with a suffix that reflected that fact. As
was true for ancient Hebrew, written vowel sounds were omitted from
ancient Egyptian hieroglyphic words, and so the precise pronunciation
of these words can often be uncertain. From this viewpoint, the association that Budge makes between Ga nu sa Ast (our Het Penu Sa Ast) and
Panopolis could suggest that the proper ancient pronunciation for the
term might have actually been *Penu-polis,* to honor the shrew mouse
deity who was celebrated there.

If, as we did with the first archaic temple name, we were to interpret
the name Het Penu Sa Ast from a cosmological perspective, we know
that Sa refers to Orion and Ast to Sirius. So the question arises as to
which astronomical body or feature we should associate with the term
penu, one that would also align in a sensible astronomical triad with
Orion and Sirius. The most obvious choice based on our understanding of the cosmology would be Barnard's Loop, the spiraling birthplace
of stars in the macrocosm that we believe correlates to the Dogon egg
of the world in the microcosm. From that perspective, the likely symbolic pairing with a mouse or a rat would likely center on the tail of
the rodent and the elephant's trunk, each of which curls into a coil and
resembles the spiral of Barnard's Loop. In all of the mythic traditions
that honor him, Ganesha's elephant's head was understood not to have
been his original head; he obtained it as a later acquisition. This change
in symbolism would have had the advantage of overtly associating a very
large animal (an elephant) with a process of the macrocosm, rather than
a tiny mouse. However, the relationships we cite to Panopolis in Egypt
suggest that the original symbolism might well have been to a mouse or
a shrew mouse.

In support of this view of the symbolism of the term *penu,* I found
another word entry in Budge's dictionary for "shrewmouse," pronounced
affi. This word is formed on the phonetic root *af,* which means "turn,
twist, revolve." These are all definitions that would be consistent with

the spiral of Barnard's Loop.[6] In further support of the view that Penu/
Ganesha was meant to symbolize what is essentially the spiral of matter that forms from waves, Snodgrass tells us that in the Buddhist
tradition, "The ancestral elephant emerged from the Waters at their
churning." He also says, "Elephants represent the Waters on which the
temple, as the embodiment of the cosmos, floats."[7] In my view, the leg-
lifting dancing position that is often taken by figures of Ganesha could
be symbolic on one level of the complex pivoting of matter that is said
to occur as waves transition into particles, a concept that is central to
our interpretation of the cosmology of ancient China.

A. K. Narain writes in an essay called "Ganeśa: A Protohistory of the
Idea and the Icon" that associations between the elephant and notions
of wisdom and learning center on the concept of Ganapati, a title for
Ganesha that defines him as the Lord of a group of enlightened devo-
tees of Buddhism. These associations originated in archaic times that
predated the Vedic tradition. He says that they were related to agrarian
rites and the domestication of animals, and originated in a time when
the images of various animals, including elephants and bulls, had been
closely associated with human activities.[8] Narain tells us that in certain
regions of India (in fact, those situated nearest to where Gobekli Tepe is
located) the elephant deity was traditionally associated with mountains
and was popularly represented by formless stones. Narain believes that
the most obvious symbolic features of an elephant are its face, its trunk,
and its tusks. He writes, "Thus the origin of Ganeśa's most striking feature, his elephant's face, must be sought in the northwest (or the north
in general), where elephants are associated with mountains (or rocks or
stones)."[9]

In Buddhism, elephants are traditionally (if somewhat counterin-
tuitively) associated with the sky, and the Celestial Elephant is said to
have had seven trunks, symbolism that again calls to mind the egg of
the world's seven rays. The Dogon refer to this "egg," which is our counterpart to Barnard's Loop in the microcosm, as the *po pilu*. Knowing
that, it is interesting that a Dravidian ethnic group in India called the

Tamil refer to Ganesha by one of their words for "elephant," which is also pronounced *pilu*.[10] In Aramaic the word for "elephant" is *pil,* and in the modern Turkish language it is *fil.* Robert L. Brown tells us that the Dravidian word may well be related to the Sanskrit word *pilusara.* Interpreted in terms of our familiar cosmological root phonemes, the compound term *pilu sa ra* could be interpreted as "elephant of Orion and the sun."

Tibetan Buddhism upholds the view that Ganesha, who according to some myths was the first son of the god Shiva, was originally depicted with an alternate head. The Tibetans say that he was later "decapitated," and his head was replaced with that of a white bull elephant called Airavata. The name comes from the Sanskrit term *iravat,* meaning "produced from water," which refers to his emergence from the churning ocean, as attested in the myths of various traditions.[11]

Once I became aware of the apparent duality of archaic temple names, and knowing of the apparent sanctuary status of the Giza plateau, it made sense to examine the phonetics of the word Giza, especially because the word begins with the same "g" sound that I considered to be an archaic form. None of Budge's words for Giza offered me any real insights into the possible symbolism of the word, but I was also aware that Dogon and Egyptian cosmological terms often seem to combine predefined phonetic root words to create more complex terms. So I turned my search toward the two phonetic roots of the word, *gi* and *sa. Gi* is an Egyptian word that refers to a "high place" or a "terrace,"[12] two attributes that can be seen to define a plateau. The term *terrace* is used as a cosmological key word in Buddhism to refer to a stupa shrine. *Sa* is a word that Budge defines to mean "knowledge deified." Taken together, these phonetic roots conveyed a meaning of "terrace of knowledge deified," a definition that seemed wholly appropriate to the likely symbolism of the Giza plateau.

The combined glyphs of the two words produced a term that was an outward match for my first two archaic temple names and began with the same archaic shrine glyph. Working again to modernize what I saw as an archaic pronunciation, I read the term alternately as Het Yah Ar Sa, where Yah represented the god of light. Budge lists a word for "light" that he pronounces *aau* or *aur* and that could be a potential correlate to the name Yah. Budge compares this to a Hebrew word for light, *aur,* that appears in the biblical book of Genesis in the signature phrase of the Hebrew god Yah, who says, "Let there be light." The word begins with the reed-leaf glyph that we already associate with the name Yah and defines an unpronounced trailing glyph, which is the light glyph 𓇶. Symbolically it reads "that which grows from the spiral." Looked at from this perspective, the Hebrew god Yah would be symbolic of the concept of light that is associated with the Dogon egg of the world and, by correlation, with the spiral of Barnard's Loop.

Figure 5.4. Egyptian word *aau*
(see Budge, *Egyptian Hieroglyphic Dictionary,* 31a)

The phoneme *ar* referred to Isis and Nephthys and thus symbolized Sirius, while *sa* referred to the god of knowledge, a term that could also relate to Osiris/Orion, who in Egyptian mythology was associated with the introduction of civilizing skills. Symbolically that would make Giza a temple of enlightenment, authority, and deified knowledge. Based on astronomical associations with these phonetic values it could again be seen as a temple to Barnard's Loop, Sirius, and Orion.

We have mentioned that one emerging concept in the field of linguistics is the notion of ultraconserved words, words that because of their significance tend to remain in a language for very extended periods of time.[13] We have also said that such words have been pivotal to our studies of regions such as China, where symbols and symbolic concepts preceded any surviving written texts. My friend Ed Nightingale, a master woodcarver from Pennsylvania, has done a great deal of good work to effectively reverse-engineer a compelling geometric plan for the Giza plateau. This plan is defined in relation to values that we associate with the famous Greek academic Plato, called Platonic numbers and ratios. So it is of particular interest that the Turkish word for "terrace" is pronounced *plateau*. However, it is actually spelled P-L-A-T-O.

Continuing with our analysis of the term Giza, the Dogon word *sa* also offers some interesting implications for our understanding of Giza as a theoretical repository of knowledge. One Dogon word *sa* means "to pass something from hand to hand," which is consonant with the idea of handing down knowledge between generations. If we entertain the perspective that Egypt exemplified a culture that might possibly have arisen just following a global catastrophe, then Giza could also represent what Calame-Griaule refers to as a very important cosmological concept: the triumph of life over death.[14]

The idea of a sanctuary is one that has always been intimately associated with ancient Egypt. In fact, one ancient name for Egypt was Khem or Khemet, a phonetic term that Budge says also means "sanctuary." In his dictionary, Budge gives several alternate glyph spellings for the word. Symbolically, the first of these spellings reads "source of knowledge," followed by the image of a shaped stone slab that would be appropriate to a sanctuary or a shrine.

Figure 5.5. Egyptian word *khem*, which means "sanctuary"
(see Budge, *Egyptian Hieroglyphic Dictionary*, 546b)

Another of Budge's spellings repeats the same symbolic sentence, "source of knowledge," only this time followed by three similarly shaped stone slabs or stone viewing slots. The symbolism of the number three calls to mind our archaic sanctuary names that appear to take their definition from three deities or cosmological concepts.

Figure 5.6. Egyptian word *khem*, second spelling
(see Budge, *Egyptian Hieroglyphic Dictionary*, 546b)

Significantly, this same phonetic value, *khem*, forms the root of the Egyptian word *khemt*, which actually means "three," and so would seem to affirm an underlying rationale for the association of a temple or sanctuary with three deities and for the otherwise possibly confusing three stone slabs that appear in the spelling of the word that means "sanctuary."[15]

This Egyptian word *khem* defines several important concepts that are integral to the creation tradition and more specifically to the Dogon conception of that tradition. For example in the Dogon language, the word *dogon* itself defines the two explicit obligations of an initiate or priest, as discussed in chapter 4: "to complete the words" and "to feign ignorance." Similarly, the Egyptian word *khem* (which as we mentioned was an ancient name for Egypt) can also mean "to bring to an end" or "to feign ignorance," and so reflects the same essential symbolism as the word *dogon*. The word *khem* also can mean "to observe, to think, to think out a matter," another of the main tasks of an initiate within the Dogon esoteric tradition.

The word *khem* can also refer to a "god of procreation and generative power," and so reflects two of the central creational themes of the cosmology. In accordance with these themes, Budge defines the word *khemenu* as a name for "the eight elemental deities of the company of Thoth," who are likely correlates to the eight symbolic ancestors associated with the Dogon egg-in-a-ball figure. The notion of ancestors, we may recall, is thought to play an important symbolic role at the sanctuary of Gobekli Tepe. Budge also says that the word *khema* can mean "to grasp," a symbolic concept that relates commonly to vultures at Gobekli Tepe and to the Amma-like creator-gods of later traditions.

Figure 5.7. Egyptian word *khema,* which means "to grasp" (see Budge, *Egyptian Hieroglyphic Dictionary,* 547b)

There are also several Turkish words that could have significance in relation to ancient Egypt or the word *khem.* For example, Budge defines a word *khemes,* which means "ear of corn." The Turkish word for Egypt, Misir, comes from a root that also means "corn." Similarly, if we subscribe to the viewpoint of Robert Bauval, the alignment of the pyramids at Giza testifies to the significant role played by the three belt stars or girdle of the constellation Orion in relation to ancient Egypt. Similarly, the Turkish term *kemer* means "belt" or "girdle." In that same regard, the enigma that is presented by the structures on the Giza plateau may be reflected in the Turkish term *giz* or *gizem,* which means "secret, mystery, or enigma."

6

Turkish and Archaic Word Forms

Because of the historical importance of the Gobekli Tepe site and the range of symbolic images and objects that it comprises, we realize that the modern-day Turkish language itself represents another potential source of information for our interpretations in this study. Our own experience throughout this series of books, commensurate with the concept of ultraconserved words, has been that ancient terms of cosmology tend to hold their meanings across cultures and languages, and, as our examples illustrate, also apparently across the many eons. I attribute this significant attribute of cosmological words to the very insightful design of the original civilizing plan. We know that this persistence of language is likely to have been an intentional feature of the system because such very great emphasis is placed on the concept of the Word within the tradition itself.

It is only fitting that the first Turkish word that we interpret to have meaning for our tradition is *adam,* a term that can mean "bird," "dog," and "man." This meaning seems appropriate in that the Turkish word *kobekli* also means "of the dog." In the tentative view we have adopted of Gobekli Tepe as the mythical "first place" of mankind's civilizing instruction, ancestral teachers, who are widely associated in many ancient traditions with Sirius, the Dog Star, were brought together with pastoral-age humanity in a locale that was overtly presented in relation to vultures and other birds. Arguably, the first known people of civilized status would have been the product of this confluence, and the memory of that collaboration seems to have carried forward in numerous ancient traditions in relation to the name Adam.

Another bird image that is closely associated with our creation tradition is that of a hawk or a falcon. We recognize this bird as the symbol of Horus in Egypt, but if we were true to our own view of how meaning is conveyed by ancient Egyptian hieroglyphic words, it also represents the concept of a symbol, since the glyph appears as the unvocalized trailing glyph of two Egyptian words, *ashem* and *akham,* which each mean "symbol."

Figure 6.1. Egyptian word *ashem*
(from Scranton, *Cosmological Origins,* 41)

Figure 6.2. Egyptian word *akham*
(from Scranton, *Cosmological Origins,* 41)

In relation to the possibly cosmological symbolism of Gobekli Tepe, the Turkish word *gebe* means "pregnant" and *gebelik* "pregnancy," meanings that call to mind the expanded womb that is symbolically associated with aligned ritual shrines in our tradition. The Turkish word *gebe* can also mean "to impregnate," which is the act that initiates biological creation, one of the central creational themes of the cosmology. The Egyptian term *bekh,* formed from a similar phonetic root, means "to give birth, to produce."[1] From this same perspective, the Turkish word *gobek* is the navel or umbilicus, and *gobekli,* which as we said is conventionally translated as "potbelly," could reasonably imply an impregnated womb.

In possible relation to the civilizing plan, the Turkish word *becki* means "guardian," "caretaker," or "watcher," terms that are sometimes associated with ancestor-teachers in our creation tradition. Bak is the Egyptian name for a "god of letters" who was one of seven wise gods, and it is also an Egyptian word for "hawk." The Egyptian word *bekhen-t* refers to "two pylons of a tower," one of the structures comparable to our shrine with the viewing slot that facilitated astronomical observations made by "watchers."[2]

Over the course of thousands of years, the priests of the Dogon tribe have shown themselves to be among the most faithful messengers of these ancient symbols and meanings. We also know that the grand mnemonic symbol of the Dogon and Buddhist traditions is the ritual shrine, which is traditionally oriented or aligned toward the east. So it seems fitting that the Turkish term for a hawk or falcon is pronounced *dogan* and that its likely phonetic root, *dogu,* means "to orient, east, and eastward." The Dogon priests believe that the ancestral dwelling place of the Dogon tribe was near a large lake located somewhere far to the east of their present-day home in southern Mali. Also supportive of these linguistic relationships is the Turkish word *gundogumu,* meaning "sunrise," a concept that is also synonymous with the direction of east in many ancient traditions.

We have discussed ways in which the Dogon egg-in-a-ball figure defines the cardinal points of space in relation to an axis. Adrian Snodgrass describes a tradition in Buddhism that associates the colors of the rainbow with spatial symbolism as a kind of color wheel that is an effective match for the Dogon egg-in-a-ball figure. It is based on a circle that has also been divided into four quadrants by two axes. In regard to color, the diffracted image of a rainbow represents the full spectrum of visible light, and so could be said to relate to the concept of light in its totality. In this Buddhist figure, the color white, which is deemed to contain within itself all of the other colors of the rainbow, is associated with the same center point of the circle that defines the creator-god Amma in the Dogon egg-in-a-ball figure. The other primary colors are set out in relation to this central point, with red, blue, and yellow plotted at the cardinal points of east, north, and south, respectively. The color green, which we know from an artistic perspective is a mixture of the colors blue and yellow, is associated with the fourth cardinal point of west and is appropriately situated halfway between blue/north and yellow/south. Conceptualized in this way, all other visible colors radiate from white in the figure, in much the same way that the material universe is said to radiate from Amma in the Dogon tradition.[3]

One Egyptian word for "white," *ubekh,* forms the root of the term Ubek-t, which Budge defines as the name of a temple to Isis and Nephthys, the two goddesses we associate with the Sirius stars.[4] By association, these references would seem to also place Sirius at the conceptual center of the color wheel. Another Egyptian word for "white" is *hetch-t,* which is defined symbolically in terms of the Egyptian sun glyph, a circle with a central dot, and so aligns conceptually with the Buddhist concept of the color wheel.[5] This word serves as a phonetic root for the word *hetchi-t* and the name of the Egyptian "white goddess" Nekhebit, whom Budge defines as a vulture goddess. These words both begin with the phonetic root *het* that we associate with our archaic temple names and with the word *hetes,* meaning "shrew mouse." The root *hetch* is often found in Egyptian words that relate to the concept of light and brightness.

The Turkish word for "bustard" (a type of vulture) is *toy kuso,* meaning "green bird." It is also interesting that each of the Turkish, Egyptian, and Dogon words for "yellow" can also mean "pale," a term that serves as a defining reference for the Dogon cosmology, which is given by Griaule and Dieterlen in relation to a pale fox. Colors also seem to play a symbolic role in Turkish language, a fact that is worthy of mention. For example, in the conceptual metaphor that the Dogon

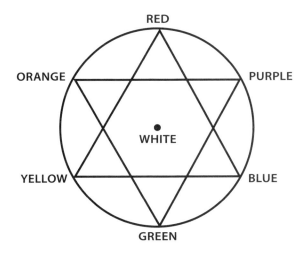

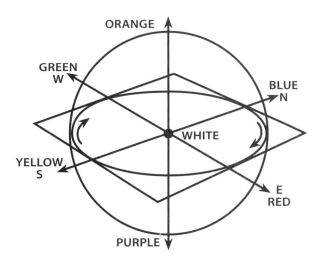

Figure 6.3. Buddhist color-wheel figures
(from Snodgrass, *Symbolism of the Stupa*, 287).

priests offer to define the four stages in the construction of a building, the final stage of completion is called *toy* or *toymu*. We have said
that this word corresponds to an Egyptian word, *temau*, which means
"complete." *Toy* is the Turkish name for the color green, the same color
that is assigned to the fourth cardinal direction of west (the direction in
which the sun sets) to complete a wheel whose first three points relate

to the primary colors. A comparable word, *tam,* is the Turkish word for "complete."

In the Turkish language the word for "white" is *ak,* a likely phonetic counterpart to the Egyptian root *akh,* which is the basis for the Egyptian word for "light," *aakhu.* This is the same phonetic value that we associate with the Dogon word *ogo,* which is also the name of the character who plays the role of light in Dogon mythology and whose actions are credited with having evoked our material universe. So based on the color wheel defined by Snodgrass, we could make a case that the concept of "white" or "light" in the Turkish language is given and understood in the same essential terms as it is in our plan of cosmology.

The Turkish word for a "star" is *yildiz,* and the term for the very bright Dog Star, Sirius, is *akyildiz,* or "white star," a symbolic reference that, by association, would again place Sirius at the conceptual hub of the Buddhist color wheel. Similarly, the Turkish word for "father" is *baba,* and the term for "vulture" is *akbaba,* or "white father." Budge defines an Egyptian name for Isis/Sothis (Sirius) based on a similar *ak* root, Aakhhu-t, which from our perspective takes an archaic form and is written with glyphs that begin with the head of a vulture. These commonalities of color symbolism would seem to associate Sirius with vultures in ancient Egypt.[6] The Dogon term *sigi* is the name of their fifty-year festival of Sirius, the whitest, brightest star in the night sky. We have often said that we identify this Dogon word with the Egyptian word *skhai,* meaning "to celebrate a festival." One Turkish word for "light" is *isik* or *isigi.* Likewise, the Turkish word for "sanctuary" is *siginak,* and the term for "worship" is *saygi.*

The Turkish word for "scorpion," another creature whose image is pictured at Gobekli Tepe, is *akrep.* We know that the Turkish word *ak* means "light" and *rep* means "hand." This construction calls to mind the ancient concept of the cubit, a unit of measure that is given in relation to a bent arm and a hand, and whose name in ancient Egypt was *aakhu meh,* and so was expressed in phonetic terms of the Egyptian word for light, *aakhu*. The scorpion is a creature whose body is largely defined by bent arms.

There are other suggestive commonalities between Turkish and Dogon cosmological words. For instance, the Turkish word for "mother" or "earth mother," *ana,* is a close phonetic match for the Dogon and Na-Khi word *na,* which means "mother." The Turkish word for "creation," *atama,* suggests the name of the Dogon creator-god Amma, and the cosmologically related concept of knowledge is expressed by the Turkish word *analama.* The concept of nonexistence is given in the Turkish language as *olmama.*

In Dogon cosmology, the term *sene* refers to a category of seedlike components of matter comparable to protons, neutrons, and electrons. The drawing that accompanies the Dogon priests' discussion of the concept of the sene is a close match for one of the patterns that an electron makes as it orbits the nucleus of an atom. The Turkish word *sene* refers to a "year," a period of time that is defined by the orbit a planet makes around its sun, which is conceptually similar to the orbit of an electron around an atom.

There are numerous resemblances that exist between Turkish words and words in Hebrew. To cite a few, the Turkish word for "universe," *alem,* calls to mind the Hebrew *olam.* The Turkish word for "circumcision" is *mitzvah,* the term for any commanded good act in Judaism, of which circumcision is one. The Turkish word for "spirit," *ruh,* is comparable to the Hebrew word *ruach.* The Turkish word *cabala* means "mystery," much as the Hebrew word *kabbalah* refers to "hidden wisdom." A Hebrew word for "charity," *sedaka,* compares favorably to the Turkish word *sadakat,* meaning "loyalty, fidelity, allegiance, or devotion." Likewise the Turkish word *sira,* which means "order, sequence, or progression," compares to the esoteric concept of *n'sirah* in Judaism that relates to the progressive stages of creation.

As we have mentioned, another unanticipated new source of information for our studies, similar to these Turkish words, is provided by what we view as archaic Egyptian word forms, comparable to Budge's name Getpetkai. From our perspective, any written Egyptian word that exhibits the shrine glyph is likely to be an archaic form, and the structure of these words often fail to conform to the familiar conventions we have defined in our studies of Egyptian cosmological words. For example, whereas we have come to expect Egyptian words to express their meanings through symbolic sentences that are sometimes followed by determinatives and/or one or more seemingly defined glyphs, many of these archaic words appear to follow a different set of conventions.

In one of these apparent conventions, the archaic word form begins with a pair of glyphs: the shrine glyph, 𓉴, and the kite glyph, 𓅝. Based on numerous examples from Budge's dictionary, these seem to signal that the word's meaning is to be understood contextually in relation to the image that is depicted by the glyph or glyphs that immediately follow this introductory pair. As examples, Budge defines the word *ga* to mean "throwing stick, boomerang," written as 𓉴𓅝𓏤,[7] and the word *gan* to mean "helpless": 𓉴𓅝𓄿𓀉.[8] This same convention seems to be conveyed in an alternate way when the standing foot glyph, 𓂾, is used in place of the kite glyph, as in the word *geb,* meaning "arm": 𓉴𓂾𓂝.[9] In both of these examples, the trailing glyph can be seen to depict the intended meaning of the word.

Similar phonetic word values are given by Genevieve Calame-Griaule in *Dictionnaire Dogon,* such as the word *gana,* or *ganu,* meaning "space" or "world." Calame-Griaule specifically comments that the word is understood to be an archaic form, as we surmised its Egyptian counterparts might be. We can demonstrate commonality for these Dogon and Egyptian words based on the word *ga,* which for the Dogon can be used as a suffix to imply obstacles or difficulties or as a word that means "to introduce an opposition." A homonym for this word means "to turn upside down," particularly in regard to the notion of capsizing in water.[10] The Egyptian term *ga* means "to overturn," and it is expressed using a glyph that reflects the image of an upturned boat: 𓊛. Like the Dogon suffix *ga,* Budge tells us that an Egyptian homonym *ga* means "to be in sore straits or great need, to suffer want, or to be obstructed."[11]

In accordance with these cross-confirming definitions and in support of our view that the archaic Egyptian word Ga nu sa Ast was likely carried forward in the traditions of India as the name of elephant-god Ganesha, one traditional role of Ganesha in ancient Indian mythology was either to introduce or remove obstacles, depending on the relative deservedness or undeservedness of the person involved.

At the time of the publication of *The Pale Fox,* Griaule and Dieterlen characterized the Dogon language as technically unclassifiable because it combines many separate but coherent subsets of words from various other languages and dialects. Our studies in cosmology uphold that view, in that they correlate an entire body of Dogon cosmological words to the ancient Egyptian hieroglyphic language and suggest that other more archaic terms may actually correspond to ancient Turkish words. Many of these same words, pronounced in an alternate way, also appear to have been ancestral to more modern Egyptian word forms. In recent years, the Foundation for Endangered Languages conducted an extensive survey of Dogon languages in Mali and concluded, "Classification of the Dogon languages is a matter of considerable dispute. They have always been considered part of [the] Niger-Congo [family of languages], but their place in that family is difficult to determine . . . [it is] estimated there are no less than 17 languages under the Dogon rubric and that the family is highly internally divided."[12]

7

The Sakti Cult
in Orissa

As a follow-up to my interpreted reading of the temple name Het Penu Sa Ast, I continued to search for references to ancient ceremonial centers or deities whose names might include the word *penu*. What I turned up were references from a region of India called Orissa to an exceedingly ancient pair of sister goddesses named Dharni Penu and Tana Penu. These deities are referred to as the Sakta (pronounced "Shakta") goddesses; they are associated with the Sakti cult, their worship dates from an era prior to Vedic times, and they are considered to have been ancestral to the Vedic, Hindu, and Buddhist traditions. The true extent of the Sakti cult's influence is difficult to define, and there are upward of a thousand different localized names or titles that can be assigned to the feminine energy that characterizes it. The tradition is thought to have been originally associated with a mountain goddess. Traces of Sakta worship are found all across India, and most often in the myths, a goddess named Sati is identified as the first wife of the god Siva. Various aspects of the mother goddess are reflected in the multiple names that were assigned to these goddesses, some of whom were portrayed as benefactors and other as destroyers. Ernest A. Payne states in his book *The Saktas: An Introductory and Comparative Study* that these surrogates of the mother goddess include one called Uma, "whose characteristics are gracious," and that a connection is possible to the great mother goddess of the Dravidians, whose name was Amma.[1]

My primary source of information about this earth mother cult comes from a book by Francesco Brighenti called *Sakti Cult in Orissa,* an exhaustive study that touches on many different aspects of the goddesses and various practices of their tradition. Based on references given in the book, the author seems to be largely unaware of Dogon culture, and he makes no mention of it in his study. However, the book has proved to be especially helpful to my comparative work because Brighenti shows himself to be a very faithful and comprehensive reporter of many aspects of the cult. He takes great care to present alternate definitions for significant words of the tradition, touches on seemingly obscure symbolic references, and is true to his sources even in situations where he admits to not being certain why a given reference pertains. My experience has been that it is within these seemingly obscure aspects of a tradition that the most useful correlative information is often found.

For a comparative cosmologist like myself, any pair of ancient sister goddesses like Dharni Penu and Tana Penu cannot fail to suggest the binary stars of Sirius, and so my first inclination was that these goddesses might represent cosmological counterparts to the sisters Isis and Nephthys in Egypt. In Egypt, Isis is traditionally associated with Sothis/Sirius, and references to her dark sister Nephthys are suggestive of the dark twin star of Sirius that was known to the Dogon. Turning once again to dictionaries as an important reference source, I learned that the word *dharni* means "luminous" and that *tana* is a reference to the "earth," a term that is synonymous in our cosmology with "mass or matter." Those meanings support an outlook from which Dharni Penu could reasonably be associated with the luminous star Sirius A, and the earth mother Tana Penu with the massive dwarf star Sirius B. Although in its earliest days the Sakti tradition, like that of the modern-day Dogon, was aniconic, meaning that its practitioners did not make iconic images of their deities, Brighenti tells us that in later eras, Tana Penu was traditionally pictured in association with a throne, the same object that was traditionally associated with Isis/Sirius in ancient Egypt.[2]

Brighenti also expresses his belief that animals played the role of determinatives in the Sakti tradition. The various animals that were traditionally associated with Sakta deities served as unique identifiers for those deities. Once iconic images of deities began to be made, the consistent presence of a deity's avatar, or *vimana,* served to effectively "lock in" later interpretations of which deity was actually pictured.[3]

We may recall that Budge's archaic name for the temple that we interpret as Het Penu Sa Ast was Ga nu sa Ast, a term that we associated with the later Buddhist god Ganesha based on archaic associations with the shrew mouse. Brighenti says that in myth, the Sakta mother goddesses actually invoked Ganesha and are invariably pictured with Ganesha in later sculptures.[4] Through the linguistics of his traditional titles, Ganesha is also suggestively linked to the Sakta earth goddesses. An early Sanskrit lexicon called the *Amarakosha* lists eight synonyms for Ganesha. Included among these is the title Dvaimatura, meaning "one who has two mothers," and another, Heramba or Lambodara, meaning "one who has a potbelly."[5] Brighenti also informs us that, in India, the word *penu,* or *pinnu,* later took on the generic meaning of "deity."[6]

The identification of the Sakta goddesses with the term *penu,* along with their very remote period of origin, suggested possible linkage to various archaic elements we find at Gobekli Tepe. In support of that perspective, Brighenti tells us that the goddesses were intimately associated with mountains, the concept of a sacred mountain, and mountain sanctuaries or shrines that were built on hilltops.[7] Likewise, the earliest aniconic objects associated with Dharni Penu were three-stone cairns topped by a fourth flat stone,[8] large stones, stone circles, and the placement of upright monoliths meant to symbolize ancestors.[9] (Common symbolism shows the cairn to be an early symbolic predecessor to a Buddhist stupa, and on page 494 of *The Pale Fox,* Marcel Griaule includes a photo of three similar Dogon stones, topped by a fourth flat stone.) Brighenti

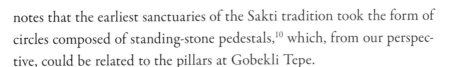

notes that the earliest sanctuaries of the Sakti tradition took the form of circles composed of standing-stone pedestals,[10] which, from our perspective, could be related to the pillars at Gobekli Tepe.

Another symbol of the mother goddess in the Sakti tradition was that of a clay pot filled with water that symbolized a womb. This pot was called a *potbelly* and was symbolic of cosmogonic transformation and fertility. We recall based on our explorations of Turkish words that "potbelly" is one of the translated meanings that is traditionally associated with the term *gobekli*. In later eras of the Sakti cult, the concept of the pot was supplanted by that of an actual womb, the same familiar symbol we interpret to have comparable meaning in the Dogon, Buddhist, and Egyptian traditions.[11]

Just as the Dogon tradition places the creator-god, Amma, symbolically at the center of the egg in a ball, the goddess of a type of divine energy that is also called Sakti also stood conceptually at the center of these stone pedestal circles. Similar archaic Buddhist shrines called *chaityas* dating from around the first century BCE consisted of a circle of standing pillars that surrounded a stupa.[12] Again as in the Dogon tradition, the center of the circle of pillars symbolized the axis mundi.[13] And as this axis was associated with a world tree in Dogon cosmology, so the Sakti tradition also associated a symbolic tree with the concepts of fertility and generative power.[14] Likewise, the Sakta three-stone cairn was associated with an ancestress who was deemed to have brought skills of agriculture, much as ancestors associated with the aligned Dogon granary are said to have brought agricultural skills to the Dogon.[15]

In this Sakti tradition, and again like the Dogon tradition we have pursued, animals came to be associated with vital forces of nature. A similar symbolic emphasis on animals seems to be reflected in the carved stone images that characterize Gobekli Tepe.[16] Likewise, the Sakti tradition placed conceptual significance on the four classic primordial elements found in many of our traditions, but some other cultures, such as that in ancient China, also added a fifth element. In the case of the Sakti tradition, this fifth element was identified as ether.[17]

Brighenti presents a list of significant contributions he feels were made by this pre-Vedic Sakti cult to later Hinduism and Buddhism. These include an emphasis on a feminine principle within the tradition, the principle of dualism, the practice of making ritual pilgrimages to temples or sanctuaries, the impulse to substitute alternate forms of worship for more ancient ritual sacrifice practices, the observance of fertility rites, and the introduction of the yogic tradition.[18] In regard to yoga, Brighenti associates this practice, carried out by a subcult of female yoginis, with the Sakta tradition. He states that from one perspective, early stone circles may have been symbolic of these yoginis, who traditionally sat in a circle. Brighenti describes the yoginis in terms that are comparable with the Dogon system of initiates and with Dogon priests, who were even called by a comparable term, *hogon*. He credits the yoginis with having preserved an esoteric tradition.[19]

As the Dogon priests do for their ancestor/teachers, Brighenti associates the Sakta goddesses with specific civilizing skills whose combined effect was to raise humanity upward from the level of hunter-gatherers to the level of farmers. These instructed disciplines can be seen to have been important to the establishment of agriculture and included such skills as the cultivation of wheat, the domestication of animals, the introduction of metalworking skills, and the earliest beginnings of stone masonry and pottery.

Like the mythical ancestor-teachers of Dogon culture, the Sakta goddesses were associated with serpents and with knowledge. Brighenti reports that in the Sakti tradition, serpents personified primeval wisdom and divine knowledge and were symbols of bio-cosmic transformation, and so came to be associated with notions of life and death. In his view, the Veda itself is considered to have been a form of the doctrine of the serpent and was understood to have been that within Buddhism.[20] The Naga, or mother serpent, was regarded as a type of deity who bestowed the benefits of fertility and healing on humanity. The Naga was considered to be aquatic and symbolized a principle of primeval sanctity that was concentrated in the primordial element of water.[21] As a reflection of the influence of this same aspect of the archaic Sakti cult on later traditions in India, all of the divine benefits provided to humanity in Hinduism were referred to as *saktis*.[22]

The cosmic powers of generation that Brighenti associates with the serpent in the Sakti tradition also have a symbolic relationship to a fish, but from Brighenti's perspective, these two animals do not outwardly relate to one another. However, we know based on the cosmic symbolism of the Dogon tradition that the fish and the serpent each symbolize a discrete stage in the formation of matter. The concept of the fish pertains to transformations that are said to occur when matter in its wave-like state is perceived, while the serpent relates to finished Words of matter and to the serpent-like membranes that are thought to form as a by-product of the processes of matter. Brighenti says that in his view the symbol of the fish has had cosmogonic associations in all epochs of the Sakti tradition.[23]

The Sakti cult embraced concepts and principles of cosmology that Brighenti sees as universal and that were originally expressed in language that moved outward with the tradition in all directions from its point of origin somewhere in western Iran or southeastern Turkey, the same general region in which Gobekli Tepe is situated.[24] He tells us that DNA and language studies indicate that the same civilizing skills that characterize the Sakti tradition spread in tandem with other elements of the tradition. From Brighenti's perspective, many of the great ancient civilizations appear to have grown out of this single archaic tradition.[25]

Reflective of that viewpoint, there is archaic symbolism that is evident in both the Sakti cult and at Gobekli Tepe that would seem to relate to Native American tribes, in much the same way that I associated the stupa-like symbolism of a Mongolian yurt with a Navaho roundhouse in *China's Cosmological Prehistory*. In the first instance, the Sakta goddesses were associated with a pole of sacrifice, to which a sacrificial animal was thought to have been tied. Poles with carved animal heads that seem outwardly similar to Native American totem poles have been unearthed at Gobekli Tepe. The Sakti poles were associated with the axis of the universe and the world tree and were considered to be a vehicle of cosmic manifestation or ascension.[26] Second, the concept of ascension is associated symbolically with the opening in the top of a yurt that is created by the internal poles that give it structure and by which it is aligned, similar to the opening at the top of a Native American tepee. A shaman whose spirit is conceptualized as moving upward through this opening is said to ascend. A third symbolic element that could reasonably relate to Native American tribes is established when Brighenti tells us that the Sakta goddesses are credited with having created the buffalo as a sacred sacrificial animal.[27]

8

Sakti References in Ancient Egypt

The Sakti tradition includes mythic storylines that can bear a striking resemblance to those that have come down to us from ancient Egypt. For example, one of the classic myths of ancient Egypt tells of how Osiris, an Egyptian god who was traditionally associated with the introduction of civilizing skills, was tricked and then murdered. Afterward, his body was said to have been dismembered and its pieces scattered across Egypt. Alternate versions of the myth credit either Osiris's wife, Isis, or their son, Horus, with recovering the scattered pieces of Osiris and reanimating him. The Sakti tradition also preserves a similar archaic myth. However, in the Sakti version it is the god Siva's wife, the goddess Sati, who is reported to have died and was then dismembered. Her body parts are said to have fallen to Earth as fifty-one *pithas,* or seats (sometimes called *pithasthanas*), which are characterized as stones. These were treated as thrones of worship, and the locations at which they fell came to be sites of ritual centers that held importance in the Sakti tradition.[1] Like Osiris, the dismembered Sakta goddess was later reconstituted or, in one version of the myth, reborn as Uma/Amma, a deity who was also identified with the goddesses Durga and Kali.[2] According to Adrian Snodgrass, in the Buddhist tradition Siva and Sati/Sakti represent the personifications of the primordial male and female principles, whose union created the cosmos.[3]

81

Perhaps the most obvious thread of Egyptian symbolism that seems to relate to the Sakta version of this myth is found in a word for "throne" or "seat," which Budge pronounces *set*. Set, of course, was also the name for the Egyptian god of evil, who is sometimes compared to the Judeo-Christian agent of evil, Satan. In his book on the Sakti cult, Brighenti also describes some of the more terrible and maleficent aspects of the Sakta goddesses, whose practices sometimes involved such things as human sacrifice, which could potentially link them with Satan.

Other possible traces of this archaic Sakti myth are also found in several Egyptian words that bear a phonetic resemblance to the term *pitha*. Budge defines the first of these, *pet-a,* as a title of Osiris. The concept of a coffin, which plays a role in the Osiris myth, could be reflected in the Egyptian word *petu-t,* meaning "chest" or "box." The notion of dismemberment could also be reflected in another Egyptian word, *peth,* which according to Budge's dictionary entry means "to tear, to rend." Yet another concept that might pertain to the myth, relating to the wide distribution of the deity's dismembered body parts, can be seen in the word *pet,* which means "to open out, to spread out, to be wide, spacious, extended," and in the word *pet[it],* which Budge gives as the uncertainly pronounced title of a sky goddess and as meaning "the spreader."[4] A similar notion of a spreading survived in Egyptian representations of the goddess Nut, whose body is depicted as spreading across the sky, and in an Egyptian glyph, ⌐══⌐, that takes the form of an overspreading arch that is traditionally interpreted to represent the concept of heaven or sky.

Brighenti tells us that Brahmanic and tribal cultures coexisted since very early times in Orissa, and so each group ultimately came to adopt aspects of the other's religion.[5] Given this cross-influence, we can understand how the concept of a cow might have come to be associated with the Sakta mother goddesses. Bulls or cows are animals whose images are depicted at Gobekli Tepe, and they were among the domesticated animals first evidenced in the same region as Gobekli

Tepe. One well-known Egyptian cow goddess is Hathor. Although the evolution of relationships among the pantheon of gods and goddesses in ancient Egypt was complex and is known to have changed over time, Hathor is considered by some researchers to have been a counterpart to or surrogate for Isis. Some actually refer to Hathor/Isis as a conceptual pairing. Others, as a way of reconciling complexities of relationships that could define Isis as both the mother and spouse of Horus, end up assigning Hathor to the lesser but still motherly role of wet nurse to Horus. Budge, however, regards Hathor as the wife of Osiris in his aspect as a bull god and as the mother of Horus. Budge even assigns Hathor, in one of her forms, the name Saait, which is phonetically similar to Sati in the Sakti tradition.[6] From this perspective, Hathor and Osiris can be seen to have held positions within the Egyptian pantheon that were comparable to those of Sati and Siva in India.

In his dictionary, Budge assigns the concept of a "sacred cow" to the term *aakhu-t,* a word formed from a root that means "light," which from a cosmological perspective implies the color white, the same color we associate symbolically with the Sakta goddesses.[7] In another dictionary entry pronounced *ka-t,* Budge defines the sister goddesses Isis and Nephthys as the "Two Cows."[8]

There were archaic symbolic associations in ancient Egypt with a mythical benben stone that is surmised to have been a meteor that fell to Earth. This is the icon that we associate with the pyramidion, the capstone at the top of an Egyptian obelisk. Looked at from our symbolic perspective on Egyptian hieroglyphic words, one entry Budge gives for the term *benben* defines the conelike glyph $\wedge$ that traditionally represents Sothis/Sirius,[9] and so also associates it with Isis and Nephthys. The Sakta goddesses were similarly identified with a meteor called the Black Stone of Mecca, which was venerated as an image of the earth mother.[10] Likewise, as I noted in chapter 7, standing stones were a very early aniconic symbol of the Sakta mother goddess, and we know that a stone that takes the same shape as the Sothis cone figure is used by the Dogon priests to represent Amma, referred to as Amma's egg.

The circle of seated yoginis in the Sakti tradition whom Brighenti links with mountaintop stone circles was also traditionally associated with the number sixty-four, numerology that Brighenti struggles to fully comprehend. However, we know that there was an ancient Egyptian technique for squaring a circle that was accomplished by correlating a circle, measured at nine units in diameter, with a square, defined with eight of the same units per side. This square marked out an area of sixty-four square units, the same approximate numerical value as the circumference of the circle.[11] So from a cosmological perspective, Brighenti's symbolism can be seen as yet another metaphor for squaring a circle, reconciling heaven and earth, or as another expression of the recurring theme of our cosmology: "as above, so below."

Several symbolic aspects that typify the Sakta goddesses are reflected in ancient Egyptian words that were formed on the phonetic root *sat* or *sata*. Budge defines a serpent goddess named Sata whose name is written with glyphs that are representations of a goose and a serpent, two animals whose images appear on the megalithic pillars at Gobekli Tepe. Sata is the same pronunciation that Budge assigns to "a mythological serpent," and so upholds our tentative correlations to Satan.

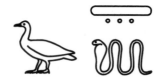

Figure 8.1. Egyptian word *sata*,
also the name of a serpent goddess
(see Budge, *Egyptian Hieroglyphic Dictionary*, 585a)

Also found on the Gobekli Tepe megaliths are images of hemispheres, a shape that combines (or reconciles) the geometric figures of a circle and a square and is given as a symbol to represent mass or matter in the microcosmic theme of our cosmology and to represent a womb in terms of the biological theme. The cosmological concept of "mass" is associated, like the Sakti goddess Tana Penu herself, with the term *earth*. Budge defines yet another word *sa-t* that actually means "earth, ground, soil, pavement."[12] Echoing the symbolism of the Sakti tradition, Budge also defines the word *ta* to mean "earth." This same phoneme is understood to mean "earth" in the cosmologies of several of the traditions we are studying. Likewise there is an Egyptian goddess, Tanen-t, the consort of Tanen, who like Tana Penu is traditionally interpreted as having been an earth goddess.[13]

Perhaps an even more direct correlation to the Sakta goddesses Dharni Penu and Tana Penu is found in Budge's word *sati*, which refers to "the two divine daughters Isis and Nephthys." These are the very same two Sirius-associated goddesses that I suggested by first impulse should associate with the Sakta sisters.[14] This word is based on the phonetic root *sa-t*, which Budge defines to mean "daughter." Budge implies that, from one mythological perspective, Isis and Nephthys were considered to be the daughters of Tem, a god whose name relates phonetically to Egyptian terms for many of the symbolic elements found at Gobekli Tepe.

Other symbolism that correlates well with the Sakta goddesses is found in the word *sa-t*, meaning "bar, bolt, beam, pillar, mast, pole" and "pillar of the earth."[15] The term also refers to "two bolts of a gate," a concept that we discovered to be central to the formation of matter in ancient China. It was our view that the Chinese symbolism was to gate hinges or bolts, whose swiveling action mimics the complex pivoting of matter that the Dogon priests say transpires immediately after a primordial wave is perceived. It is interesting that Robert Graves associates this same concept of door bolts with the white goddess of ancient Greece.

It is also telling that Budge defines a word *s-t* that means "seat, throne, place," since thrones are explicitly associated with the Sakta goddesses. Symbolically, the Egyptian word reads "throne of matter." The stones or pithas that fell to Earth when the goddess Sati was dismembered are alternately referred to as "thrones." A second Egyptian word entry of *s-t* refers to "geese," birds that are again pictured prominently in carvings on the Gobekli Tepe megaliths.

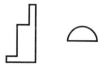

Figure 8.2. Egyptian word *s-t*,
which means "seat, throne, place"
(see Budge, *Egyptian Hieroglyphic Dictionary*, 583b)

9

Ascension

During our brief discussion at the end of chapter 7 about possible Sakti symbolism that could relate to Native American tribes, we made reference to the concept of ascension. Ascension is a topic that we have not discussed at length in any of the previous volumes of this series, but it is one that, in our view, lies very close to the heart of the traditions we study. Like other cosmological concepts that are given in terms of multiple creational themes, the notion of ascension has meaning both in relation to an individual in regard to the microcosm of matter and in relation to the larger cosmos.

On a human level, from the Buddhist perspective, the term *ascension* is interlinked with the concept of enlightenment, the idea that a devotee or inwardly examining person who dedicates himself or herself to an understanding of his or her own consciousness can attain a level of perception that will move that person to a higher spiritual plane or into a state of greater purity. This is one of the beliefs that is put forward in Buddhism, in the practice of yoga, and that is expressed in many Eastern religions.

From a microcosmic perspective, Dogon definitions of how particles of matter derive from waves are given in terms of an upward movement through three conceptual worlds via a process that is characterized as ascent. The concept of ascent is equated in some cultures with the notion of "climbing up." Budge lists a word, *sakh,* that means "to raise up, to lift up on high," and the phonetic root suggests that its meaning could well relate to our concept of ascension.[1] The word defines a glyph that is the image of a person who holds the sky or heaven glyph above his head.

Likewise, the notion of a particle, as symbolized by the image of a clay pot, is central to the Dogon phrase *toro nomo,* which means "to climb up," which is one essential definition of the concept "to ascend." The Dogon word *toro* means "pot of water," and so coincides with the concept of a "potbelly," an aniconic symbol of the Sakti mother goddess that represents a womb. In the Dogon tradition, it was the wife of the ancestral smithy who first discovered pottery when she unintentionally left a clay pot to dry in the proximity of a nearby forge. From our perspective on the symbolism of cosmological phonetics, the words *toro nomo* refer to "the clay pot of waves perceived."

A parallel concept of ascent is defined biologically in terms of the notion of a meditative spirit, soul, or energy, called *sakti,* that in the Vedic tradition moves spiritually upward through the body at the time of ascension. This energy or soul is said to emerge through one of nine bodily orifices, and its ultimate disposition depends largely on where it emerges. The soul of a fully enlightened person is said to emerge through the top of the head.

On a macrocosmic level, the concept of ascension is rooted in a tradition that holds that our material universe, like all other aspects of creation, conforms to a principle of dualism. One common perception is that when our universe formed, its emergence was paired with a second ethereal, nonmaterial, or spiritual universe, one that is largely beyond the day-to-day perception of humanity. In this regard, the Vedic tradition professes an outlook that is fundamentally similar to that of Buddhism and that is found in other ancient traditions such as the Jewish Kabbalah. In the view of the Vedics, when our universe formed it emerged hand in hand with a second paired spiritual universe. The formative difference between the two universes is expressed in a Dogon myth that describes the initial descent of eight mythical ancestors and serves as a kind of public gloss for a more detailed private explanation that is given to the most accomplished Dogon initiates.

The Dogon ancestors are defined in terms of eight ordinal civilizing Words or civilizing concepts, but after the first six Dogon ancestors descended in proper numerical sequence, the Dogon myth describes the eighth ancestor as having come down "out of order" or "out of sequence." In what was considered to be a breach of cosmic order, the eighth ancestor is said to have appeared ahead of the seventh, an act that so angered the seventh ancestor that he ostensibly killed the interloping eighth ancestor. When Marcel Griaule questioned his principal informant (the Dogon priest Ogotemmeli) about this point, the priest confessed that the myth was merely symbolic, meant to illustrate a cosmological concept, and that in reality no ancestor had actually died.

From our perspective, several Egyptian words for "anger" symbolically define a glyph that is the image of a crocodile, another animal that is pictured on the Gobekli Tepe megaliths and one that, because of its predatory habits, could reasonably symbolize the concept of anger. One Egyptian word for "anger," *hetchenu,* is given in terms of the same *het* root as Egyptian words for "temple" and "shrew mouse" and is expressed in symbols that, from a cosmological perspective, pertain to the formation of matter. The symbols used to write this word all have symbolic significance that relates to the formation of matter. Conceptually, a perceived wave (defined by the wave glyph) pivots and raises up (illustrated by the twisting spiral) to create the spoken Word of matter (symbolized by the serpent glyph). The clay pot (a particle) and the spiraling egg of the world (the Calabi-Yau space) are physical representations of that Word.[2] A second Egyptian word, *ati,* is defined by Budge as meaning "to be angry, to behave in a beastly manner."[3] By our standard, this word defines the crocodile glyph. It is also based on the phonetic root *at,* which means "crocodile."

Figure 9.1. Egyptian word *hetchenu,* which means "anger"
(see Budge, *Egyptian Hieroglyphic Dictionary,* 524b)

Beyond this public Dogon myth that touches on the notion of an inherent incongruity in the structure of our universe, the Dogon priests also explain the difference between the universes more concretely, in terms that I compare to the Japanese food sushi, a ritualized form of food that, like the Dogon egg of the world, takes the form of a spiraling coil. The Dogon priests say, in agreement with modern string theorists, that as matter forms, there is a stage at which membranes (a concept that the Dogon priests compare to the thin covering that surrounds the brain) are said to form from vibrating threads that weave matter. Conceptually, these membranes can either roll up "inside" the coil of matter like the inner spiral of seaweed in one type of sushi, or wrap around the outside like the outer wrapping of a second sushi, type. The suggestion is that the first method of coiling produces a nonmaterial universe, the second a material one.

In a more detailed explanation that is given to advanced initiates, the Dogon priests also profess an overt belief in the pairing of universes, but they carry these descriptions further than many of the other traditions we are studying. The Dogon priests say that our universe formed as one of fourteen superposed universes that, like the Dogon ancestors and the eight male and female Egyptian Ennead or Ogdoad gods and goddesses, evolved as sets of paired opposites. For the Dogon priests, the notion of paired opposites constitutes a principle of creation in the universe. The first of each pair of universes was nonmaterial (or spiritual) in nature, followed by a second substantive universe that consisted of mass and matter, comparable to our own. Griaule and Dieterlen describe the process of the formation of these universes (or "worlds") in *The Pale Fox*. The passage is given in descriptive phrases that call to mind both the expanding spiral of Barnard's Loop and the spinning dance of Ganesha.

Amma was standing at the center, spinning on his own axis, his right arm stretched out horizontally with all fingers extended; he turned from right to left, first facing west, then north, then east, then south. As he spun, he progressively lowered his arm, once every two turns. He turned fourteen times and stopped, facing west, his arm completely lowered. With each turn, Amma created "a heaven and an earth, stuck together." The spiral being conical due to the movement of Amma's arm, "the earths and the heavens of the lower portion were not as wide as those at the top. . . . Thus Amma spun (spiraled) space," spinning and dancing, Amma formed all the spiraling star worlds of the universe.[4]

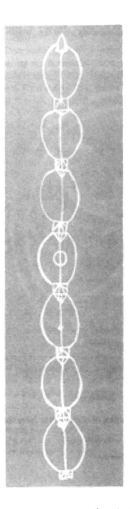

Figure 9.2. Fourteen superposed universes of Amma
(from Griaule and Dieterlen, *Pale Fox*)

One very interesting point to be observed about this description is that it is given from a perspective that is the conceptual reverse of our own Earth-based view, as if north and south had since been transposed. In modern terms, any motion that begins facing to the west and turns from right to left would next move to the south, not to the north. This discrepancy argues in favor of an Egyptian tradition, which holds that three times within the memory of Egyptian culture, the sun "rose where it formerly set." It also lends additional support for the view that the Dogon culture preserves a very early version of the ancient Egyptian tradition.

In the Dogon tradition, the seven material universes of the macrocosm are correlates to the seven wrapped-up dimensions of a Calabi-Yau space (the Dogon egg of the world) in the microcosm. These microscopic dimensions are referred to as pylons or chambers by the Dogon priests and are likely correlates to what the ancient Egyptians called *arits*. Budge tells us that there were seven arits and that each was in charge of a gatekeeper, a watcher, and a herald. In *Sacred Symbols of the Dogon* I associated the term *gatekeeper* with the connective openings between these wrapped-up dimensions, the term *watcher* with the impulse that initiates the wrapping-up of the next dimension, and the term *herald* with the repetitive spiraling loop. In ancient times the job of a herald was to travel from village to village, repeating the same message.[5] In our view of Egyptian hieroglyphic words, the Egyptian word for *arit* defines the Egyptian door glyph, and so suggests the concept of a kind of gate.

From the perspective of the Buddhist stupa tradition as expressed by Adrian Snodgrass, ascension in the macrocosm is understood in terms of a motion that rises upward from our material universe through a sun door and into the nonmaterial or Brahmanic universe. Snodgrass explains that the term *brahma* means "spiritual." According to Snodgrass, Buddhism defines three specific types of ascent in the macrocosm, which he illustrates diagrammatically with a figure that is conceptualized in relation to three domes or hemispheres. The dome symbolism is a three-dimensional extension of the circular two-dimensional color wheel discussed in chapter 6 and, according to Snodgrass, relates to the concept of a bridge. These domes correspond to instructions he gives for how to locate this macrocosmic sun door. However, Snodgrass notes that his instructions are framed in terms of a polar model, one that is based on an earthly perspective and not on the solar or cosmic model to which they are said to relate. Consequently it is left to us to transpose to the macrocosmic level the statements of symbolic import that Snodgrass gives to us in relation to the globe of the Earth.

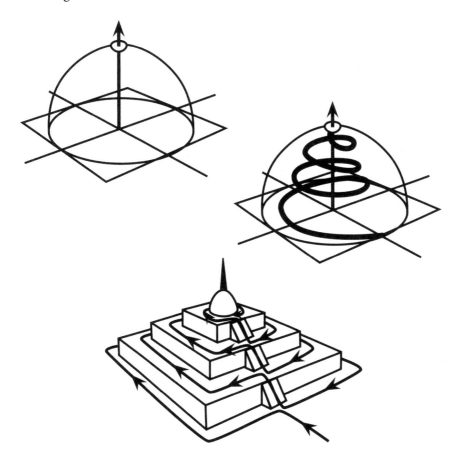

Figure 9.3. Three types of ascent in Buddhism
(from Snodgrass, *Symbolism of the Stupa,* p. 286)

Snodgrass defines a solar gate that is said to exist at the apex, or northernmost pole, of the world egg. He says that the corresponding "centre of the heavenly sphere . . . is not coincident with the physical and visible centre of the turning of the stars. The celestial sphere appears to revolve about an axis that is not vertical but set obliquely to the plane of the earth. . . . According to one mode of symbolic expression, the exit from the universe is located there, at the hub of the turning wheel of the constellations."[6]

From the standpoint of our cosmology, any reference to a "turning wheel" that relates to stars that revolve in the macrocosm suggests the motion of precession and Barnard's Loop, the spiraling structure that we interpret as the wheel of the Dogon chariot of Orion. This attribution suggests that the middle domed figure of Snodgrass's illustration, the one that can be seen to enclose a spiral, is a likely representation of Barnard's Loop.

Snodgrass says that the best way to reconcile the problem of our "oblique" perspective is to project the circular dome of the heaven onto the flat plane of the Earth and essentially square the macrocosmic circle. Metaphorically, this is what Snodgrass does when he frames his instructions for how to locate the sun door in terms of Earth-based references. From this same perspective, this concept might well be what is also represented by various squared-circle symbols defined in our cosmology, such as the mandala or the Dogon egg in the ball/ picture of Amma. Extended to three dimensions, the starting point of macrocosmic creation would be at the center point, the same conceptual point at which Amma resides, which would also be the location of Snodgrass's sun door. Snodgrass calls this "the Gateway of Exit, the doorway of escape from the cosmos." He comments, "To reach 'the summit of the universe' is also to reach its point of origin, the 'eldest' place,'" which can also mean to "become contemporary with the world's beginning."[7]

As I implied during our discussion of the term Giza in chapter 5, Budge defines an Egyptian "god of knowledge and intelligence" named Saa, a word that is based on the same phonetic values that we associate with Orion. Symbolically, this name reads "the reconciled square and circle come to be the spiral." This same pronunciation forms the phonetic root of the word *saat-t,* which Budge defines to mean "to be oblique-eyed," but that based on Snodgrass's observations we might alternately interpret to mean "to see obliquely."

Figure 9.4. Name of Egyptian god *Saa*
(see Budge, *Egyptian Hieroglyphic Dictionary,* 641a)

Since the hub is not located where one might intuitively expect to find it, Snodgrass says that we must draw a line that connects three points in order to locate it. We know that the Dogon associate Barnard's Loop with Sirius and the three belt stars of Orion, and that one direct method of locating Sirius in a darkened night sky is to draw an imaginary line through the belt stars and simply follow it downward to Sirius. Both Barnard's Loop and the massive dwarf star Sirius B are thought to have been the product of a supernova, and so the suggestion is that a single event may have created both structures. From that perspective, Sirius B would be the hub of the wheel and therefore the likely site of Snodgrass's macrocosmic gate. This conclusion makes sense in terms of Snodgrass's diagram of the three types of ascent, where the leftmost figure defines a line between two points (comparable to the two Sirius stars) and the rightmost figure defines three steps upward (or symbolically, the three belt stars of Orion).

The possibility that gates might actually exist between universes is one that is supported mathematically under the formulas of a recent theory called loop quantum gravity. From the perspective of this theory, the traditional astronomical concept of a black hole (a point in space-time that is thought to be so very massive that not even light can escape its gravitational pull) is conceptualized more as a passage-way or tunnel than as a bottomless hole. This might constitute a kind of "shortcut" between locales in our universe, or even a kind of gate-way between universes.

Snodgrass also echoes the fundamental essence of Dogon thought regarding Amma's creation of fourteen worlds when he repeats a myth from the stupa tradition that tells of how Buddha reached the summit or gate of the universe. According to Snodgrass, Buddha approached it by making seven steps, and each progressive step pointed both "upwards and downwards to indicate his preeminence in all the levels of existence, both above and below." These footsteps are conceptu-alized in the Buddhist tradition as a string of beads set out along a line that marks the axis of the cosmos and symbolizes its seven direc-tions. Snodgrass says that these steps are associated with a series of superimposed worlds (the same term used in the Dogon description) that Buddha created.[8] The concept is so remarkably similar to the one expressed by the Dogon priests that we could almost substitute Snodgrass's statement as a caption for the Dogon drawing of the four-teen paired universes of Amma.

Ancient concepts of the structure of the universe and of matter are often given in symbolic terms that echo aspects of the Dogon and Buddhist descriptions. For example, in Jainism creation is conceived of in terms of three worlds that are comparable to the three Dogon worlds of matter. The dimensions of the cosmos are given in *raijjus,* a unit of measure that is defined as "the distance a god can go in 6 months when he goes 100,000 yojanas [9 miles each] in the winking of an eye." The dimensions of the cosmos are expressed as if we were measuring a pyramid, given in terms of its height and its base. It is said to measure fourteen raijjus high, and its base to measure seven raijjus from east to west and seven from north to south.[9] In our experience with ancient cosmologies, Sirius and symbolic concepts relating to the spiritual realm are often associated directionally with the east, and those of the mun-dane world with north and south. The Jainist number fourteen, cited in relation to the cosmos and assigned in units of seven to the material and spiritual domains, mirrors the numbers that define the creation of Amma.

From a modern scientific perspective, the idea of multiple universes is one that makes sense cosmologically. In his book *Parallel Worlds,* astrophysicist Michio Kaku quotes Allan Guth, the author of the theory of an inflationary universe, as saying, "Inflation pretty much forces the idea of multiple universes upon us."[10] Brian Greene paraphrases Leonard Susskind, a theoretical physicist from Stanford University, in his 2011 book *The Hidden Reality,* stating, "Those who ignore the possibility that we're part of a multiverse are merely averting their eyes from a vision they find overwhelming."[11]

The concept of ascension is one that can also be seen to have been central to the Sakti tradition, as we might reasonably expect, since the tradition centers on two sister goddesses who seem to relate symbolically to the two Sirius stars. According to Brighenti the Vedic term *sakti* actually embodies the microcosmic concept of manifestation that we associate with ascension, defined as a female energy that causes male energy to become manifest in the cosmos.[12] Likewise on a biological level, the navel-centered energy of a person that, through inward meditation and the processes of enlightenment, is said to ascend upward through the top of the head is called sakti.

Budge includes a word entry in his dictionary that is pronounced *hi* and that means "to rise up, to ascend." This word is written with the twisted rope glyph, §, that I have associated in prior volumes with concepts of biological reproduction and DNA. However, in this context the glyph presents an image that is quite reminiscent of the Dogon drawing of the fourteen worlds of Amma, and so a relationship between the two figures also seems likely. If we interpret the word as an archaic form, presume the leading glyph to be an unpronounced defined glyph, and read the trailing glyphs of the word as a symbolic definition, then the glyphs of the word seem to imply the concept of "existence transmitted," a meaning that would be wholly appropriate both to DNA and to the similarly shaped configuration of Amma's fourteen evoked worlds.

Figure 9.5. Egyptian word *hi*,
which means "to rise up, to ascend"
(see Budge, *Egyptian Hieroglyphic Dictionary,* 468a)

In his essay "Ganeśa: A Protohistory of the Idea and the Icon," A. K. Narain discusses an image of Ganesha that is found on coin types of the Greco-Indian kings, which reflect classic symbolism that would be associated with Ganesha in later times. He mentions a Tibetan tradition that assigns Ganesha the role of a doorkeeper, the same term that we associate with the wrapped-up dimensions of the Calabi-Yau space. He says that on the reverse side of these coins there is the picture of a caduceus, consisting of two snakes entwined around Apollo's wand. Once again, this calls to mind the image of Amma's intertwined universes.

10

The Concept of Untying

In our early studies, we found that Egyptian concepts of weaving and tying proved pivotal to our understanding the processes of matter and provided an entry point to the references that define them. Now it appears that the concept of untying may play a similar role as we attempt to pull them all back together again into a single, coherent paradigm. Numerous Egyptian word references suggest that cosmological symbolism that relates to notions of heaven and earth, to Barnard's Loop, to Ganesha, to the shrew mouse, to the concept of ascension, and perhaps even to symbolic images found at Gobekli Tepe, all seem to relate to the notion of "untying." Ultimately, these words may have as much to do with helping us untangle a disparate array of cosmological concepts as with the actual processes of cosmology themselves. We will see that Budge's word definitions support each of these outlooks.

Our exploration of this concept of untying begins with the word *afekh,* which Budge defines to mean "to unloose, to untie, to unroll, to disentangle." Symbolically, the glyphs used to spell the word read "that which transmits the source." In this symbolism, we see likely references to two distinct "sources": the primordial source of the material universe and the conceptual source of the cosmological plan.

Phonetically the Egyptian word *afekh* calls to mind the modern English word *affect.* It takes its pronunciation from the phonetic root

Figure 10.1. Egyptian word *afekh,* which means
"to unloose, to untie, to unroll, to disentangle"
(see Budge, *Egyptian Hieroglyphic Dictionary,* 43b)

af, which in Budge's view means "to turn, to twist, to revolve." From a cosmological standpoint, these meanings suggest the spiral of the Dogon egg of the world and of Barnard's Loop. Symbolically, Budge's spelling of this word reads "that which transmits the spiral," and by our standard, the word defines the serpent glyph. The serpent is an animal that we associate symbolically with the Dogon Word of matter and with the spiraling egg that constitutes the first finished structure of matter.

Figure 10.2. Egyptian phonetic root *af,*
which means "to turn, to twist, to revolve"
(see Budge, *Egyptian Hieroglyphic Dictionary,* 43b)

Conceptually, Barnard's Loop is a spiraling birthplace of stars whose circular motions we relate to the concept of the precession of the equinoxes, the long, slow apparent rotation of the constellations of stars in relation to the Earth. Each of the classic ancient units of time measurement seems to have been based on a factor of this grand period of precession, the longest cycle of time that was evident from our earth-bound frame of reference. In Egypt these measures included a 360-day year, three seasons of twelve weeks each, a twelve-month year of thirty days each, a ten-day week of twenty-four hours each, and a sixty-minute hour of sixty seconds each. The Dogon modify this somewhat in that they now observed a five-day week, although the number five is still also a factor of the grand cycle of precession.

Some proponents of a controversial version of string theory called torsion theory postulate the existence of a tiny spiraling vortex at each point of space-time, comparable to the Dogon egg of the world. The theory suggests that these tiny vortices are responsible for the tug of gravity and that their effect can be countered with a reverse electromagnetic rotation. Applicable to that viewpoint, Budge lists a word *af*, which he defines as "a serpent hostile to Ra," the same Egyptian god whom we associate cosmologically with the force of gravity.[1] Symbolically it also reads "that which transmits the spiral," followed by a now-altered version of the serpent glyph, one that shows diagonal lines extending upward from each of its undulating coils.

On the same dictionary page and based on the same phonetic root Budge lists the word *affi*, which again means "shrew mouse, shrew mouse god." The symbols of this word read "that which transmits duality and existence," followed by the fish glyph. In Dogon cosmology the fish symbolizes the process by which duality comes into existence, a process that is explained in terms of the various components of the nummo fish drawing.

Figure 10.3. Egyptian word *affi*,
which means "shrewmouse, shrew-mouse god"
(see Budge, *Egyptian Hieroglyphic Dictionary*, 43b)

Farther down this same column of Budge's dictionary page we find two entries for the term *aft*, which refer to a rectangular box or sarcophagus. This was the object in the Egyptian myth of Osiris that was the vehicle for his death and dismemberment. Osiris is a god that we associate with the constellation of Orion, and Barnard's Loop—the spiral that centers on the stars of Orion's belt—is the macrocosmic counterpart to the spiral of the Dogon second world, where matter is first disrupted, then fundamentally reordered.

The next of our Egyptian "untie" words Budge gives as *atennu,* referring to an "untier of knots" or a "solver of difficulties." (Here we see a possible relationship to the English word *attenuate.*) The same word can refer to "knots" or "difficult points in a book or argument."[2] One of the traditional roles of the elephant-god Ganesha of India, the deity we associate with Barnard's Loop, was to create and remove obstacles or difficulties.

The Egyptian word *atenu,* meaning "deputy," is based on the root *aten,* which means "to act as a deputy." This is a word that we associate with the belt stars of Orion based on the Dogon tradition that defines these stars as "deputies of Sirius," which is given with the word *atanu.* Budge defines a related word, *ater,* to mean "belt of Orion."[3] Budge's term *aterti* is "the name of a funerary coffer; a shrine of Osiris."

A third set of words that reflect this same concept of "untying" is given in terms of the phonetic root *uha.* The first means "to untie, loosen, set free, release, solve a riddle, unravel a problem, separate heaven from earth."[4] A second entry under the same pronunciation means "to inspect, examine into." A third word entry for *uha* refers to a "matter which has to be explained, problem, riddle, parable." Yet another word for *uha* refers to "a builder's cord," which is the object that is often associated by traditional Egyptologists with the figure of the spiral glyph.

Yet another set of pertinent word meanings that center on the concept of "untie" are expressed by the word *mefkh.*[5] Budge defines that word to mean "untie, release, loosen." A second word, *mefkh-t,* means "to pass corn through a sieve." We mentioned in previous books that the cosmological concepts of the spiral and the manifestation of matter are compared in the Dogon tradition to the concept of a sieve.

If all of that were not enough to reflect the cosmological significance of the concept of untying in relation to various concepts we have been studying, there is another set of "untie" words that are based on the root *net,* the same term that represents the name of the Egyptian mother goddess Neith, whose role it is to weave matter. These include the word *netf,* which means to "untie, set free, loosen," and the word *neter* itself, a term that Budge says meant "god" or "God" throughout all periods of ancient Egyptian culture.[6]

Another Egyptian word, *s-thes,* is again given in terms that call to mind Ganesha in India. The definition of this word is to "unravel, untie, solve difficulty."[7] According to Budge, the word *s-fekh* means "to untie, loosen, unbind," and by our standard of interpretation defines the spiral glyph. It also means to "unbolt a door," a reference to door bolts, which we associate with the Sakta mother goddesses.[8] Another word, *sefekh,* means "seven," a likely reference to the seven rays of the egg of the world, whose endpoints define the spiral of matter.

From the Buddhist perspective, Adrian Snodgrass says that the serpent is a symbol of the upward and downward flow (or churn) of the waters that connect essence (a concept that can be associated with the Brahmanic or spiritual universe) with substance (our material universe). The diagram he gives of these ascending and descending influences is illustrated in terms of a circle inscribed within a square (a squared circle) that is divided by an axis (the axis of the universe) into four quadrants (the four primordial elements of the Dogon picture of Amma) and that is situated between the waves of the "upper waters" (above) and the "lower waters" (below). Upward and downward arrows that pass perpendicularly through the plane of the squared circle imply a process of transference in both directions.

Snodgrass explicitly associates these upward and downward movements with ascending and descending spirals (defined as *asuras* and *devas*) that uncoil (or "loosen or untie") around the axis, emanating "from the poles of the Cosmic Egg."[9] This cosmic pole is the same feature that we associated in the previous chapter with the sun door, which Snodgrass says exists and which, based on his descriptions, we place at Sirius.

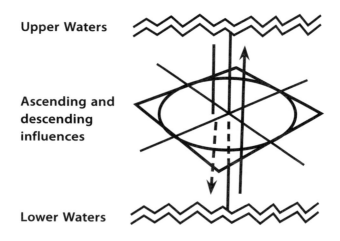

Upper Waters

Ascending and descending influences

Lower Waters

Figure 10.4. Circulation between upper and lower waters
(From Snodgrass, *Symbolism of the Stupa*, 295)

Based on these references, we can interpret the Dogon and Egyptian civic practice of establishing districts or villages in pairs called upper and lower as symbolic of this aspect of creation.

Snodgrass equates these processes of coiled "spiration" with Hindu-Buddhist symbolism that relates to "inspiration," or breath. He depicts the movement of these forces of inspiration in relation to the axis of the human body, using a heliacal figure that is a close match for the figure of the fourteen universes of Amma. Through this commonality, Snodgrass essentially correlates the concept of biological ascension and enlightenment to the same principle that the Dogon priests tell us defines the universe.

Snodgrass also equates this cycle of the upward and downward motion of the waters to the cosmological notion of a rainbow and to the earthly water cycle, in which the water that resides in lakes, rivers, and oceans evaporates to form clouds, rises upward through the atmosphere, cools, condenses, and falls as rain, and then returns as runoff to its originating bodies of water. This is the same essential concept of cosmology we defined in *The Science of the Dogon* based on Marcel Griaule's Dogon references in his work *Conversations with*

Ogotemmeli. Using a similar metaphor, the Dogon seem to define the stages of the natural water cycle in terms of a rainbow and a celestial ram. Here it seems sensible to pause and point out that the original French title of Griaule's Ogotemmeli book was *Dieu d'Eau,* or *God of Water.*

11

The Heliacal Rise
of Sirius

The term *heliacal* means "related to or near the sun," so the "heliacal rise of Sirius" refers to the annual reappearance of the brilliant star Sirius above the eastern horizon just before sunrise, following a period of time during which the star is not visible. The reason this happens is that, during the annual rotation of the Earth around the sun, the planet's position in relation to the sun and the stars changes. There is a point in this rotation where the sun is positioned between the Earth and Sirius for approximately seventy days, during which the sun's glare effectively blocks our view of Sirius. Immediately following this period of invisibility, Sirius can be seen momentarily in a darkened predawn sky as it rises above the horizon of the Earth just ahead of the sun. Sirius soon becomes invisible again due to the bright glare of the rising sun. This annual reappearance of Sirius is referred to as its heliacal rising.

At Egypt's geographic latitude, the reemergence of Sirius occurs at around the time of the summer solstice. In ancient Egypt, it was this event that signaled an annual inundation of the Nile River, caused by floodwaters that according to the ancient historian Herodotus rose for a hundred days, then receded, depositing fertile soil as they went. Flooding could be expected to occur within about a month after the rising of the star. This natural fertilizing process served to renew the nutrients of the soil and came to be relied on to promote a productive agricultural season. The regular cycle of Nile flooding is thought to have played a role in the establishment of a three-season year in ancient Egypt. Historian H. W. E Saggs writes in his book *Civilization before Greece and Rome:*

> The Nile rises and floods the land in a very uniform and predictable pattern, so that in ancient times it became thought of as dividing the Egyptian agricultural year into three seasons. The first season was the time of inundation, from when the river began to rise until it had fallen sufficiently to permit sowing. The second season was the time from sowing to harvest, and the third was the period of low water between harvest and the beginning of the next inundation. Experience showed that each of these seasons lasted about four lunar months.[1]

For both the ancient Egyptians and the Dogon (who both used the same calendar systems) it was the heliacal rise of Sirius that determined the start of the new year in relation to their solar calendar. In Egypt, the rise of Sirius is understood to have defined the start of the year at least since early in the third millennium BCE. According to R. T. Rundle Clark in his book *Myth and Symbol in Ancient Egypt,* the rising of the sun on New Year's Day symbolized the creation of the world.[2]

R. A. Schwaller de Lubicz, the great Egyptian symbolist, noted, "Owing to the precession of the equinoxes, on the one hand, and the movement of Sirius on the other, the position of the sun with respect to Sirius is displaced in the same direction, almost exactly to the same extent." Because of this, "*Sirius is the only star among the 'fixed stars' which allows this cycle.* It can therefore be supposed that Sirius plays the role of a center for the circuit of our entire solar system."[3]

In the Dogon tradition, Sirius and our sun are conceptualized as macrocosmic siblings that are said to have been born from "twin placentas." This symbolism reaffirms the outlook of the Dogon priests that our material universe emerged side by side with a nonmaterial one as a kind of twin birth. This coupling upheld a fundamental principle in the universe of dualism and the pairing of opposites. If we consider that the concept of light is functionally equated to the color white in the Buddhist color wheel, then comparable symbolism can be seen to be reflected in the Turkish language, where, as we have noted, *yildiz* means "star," *akyildiz* (or literally "white star") refers to the Dog Star, Sirius, and the terms *isik* and *isigi* mean "light" (similar to the name of the Dogon Sigi festival of Sirius); in addition, *izik* means "twin."

Like other Dogon cosmological concepts, priestly statements that relate to the heliacal rising of Sirius are supported by a cosmological drawing that is described with the phrase "Sirius meets the sun." The name that is assigned to this event is *taba tolo*. These are two words that, like many other cosmological terms, can be understood to combine other familiar cosmological prefixes and suffixes. The Dogon word *tolo* is used to identify stars and is a likely counterpart to the Egyptian word *tau,* meaning "star." The phonetic value *ta,* which we discussed in chapter 8 in relation to the name of the Sakta earth mother Tana Penu, is a cosmological term that means "earth" and that we interpret to symbolize the concept of mass, matter, or substance. In support of that view, Budge lists a dictionary entry for the name Ta, which he defines as the name of an ancient Egyptian earth god.[4] According to Genevieve Calame-Griaule, the Dogon word *ba* refers to "a temporal or spatial limit,"[5] while the Egyptian word *ba* refers to the concepts of "soul" or "spirit." If we interpret these two phonemes, *ta* and *ba,* from the perspective of the twin Dogon and Buddhist universes that these stars seem to represent, the terms "matter" and "spirit" seem to sensibly apply. From this perspective, we could interpret the Dogon term *taba tolo,* described as "Sirius meets the Sun," to mean "stars of spirit and matter."

Mythologically, in ancient times the Egyptian goddesses Isis and

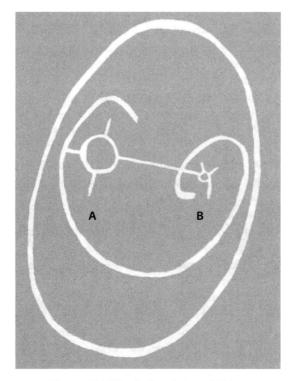

Figure 11.1. The heliacal rise of Sirius,
in which Sirius meets the sun, also known as *taba tolo*
(from Griaule and Dieterlen, *Pale Fox*, 279)

Nephthys were referred to as "the two vultures," and in some cases they seem to have been symbolized in Egyptian words by the vulture glyph, 🦅. One such word, *ner-ti,* refers to Isis and Nephthys as "vulture goddesses." According to Budge, the concept of "the opening of the year" is given by the related term *ner* or *ner-t.* This word is written with the same vulture glyph and the Egyptian sun glyph, and so symbolically conveys the same essential meaning as the Dogon term *taba tolo:* Sirius meets the sun.[6] Likewise, in his book *Ancient Egyptian Religion,* Stephen Quirke makes mention of an ancient Egyptian ceremony of "joining the sun disk" that was performed at the New Year.[7] The Egyptian term *ner* is a possible counterpart to a Dogon word *nay,* which refers to the sun, particularly in relation to the solstices.[8] These varied references seem to make clear that the Egyptians and the Dogon understood the concept of the heliacal rising of Sirius in mutual and comparable ways.

Figure 11.2. Egyptian word *ner,*
which means "opening of the year"
(see Budge, *Egyptian Hieroglyphic Dictionary,* 379a)

From another point of view, this again given from an Egyptian perspective, some researchers of Egyptian mysteries such as Graham Hancock and Robert Bauval argue that both the lion-like image and the alignment of the Sphinx at Giza were meant to point to the helia-cal rising of Sirius during a remote epoch when, because of the slow rotational cycle of precession, the star would have been seen to rise against the backdrop of the constellation Leo. The synchronization of these two astronomical events serves to associate the concept of the heliacal rise of Sirius symbolically with the Giza Plateau, where the Sphinx enigmatically reclines. So it is quite interesting that Calame-Griaule defines the Dogon word *taba* to mean "plateau."[9]

We learn from her *Dictionnaire Dogon* that the Dogon word *taba* also means "to touch with the fingers of the hand." This is symbolism that we might well associate with the enigmatic carved images of arms and hands on the megalithic pillars at Gobekli Tepe. This same mean-ing is alternately conveyed by the Dogon term *numo tabala.* Readers who are familiar with Dogon symbolism will realize that the word *numo* is one that is intimately associated with the Dogon concept of beneficent ancestral teachers.

There is evidence that the heliacal rising of Sirius held significance for other ancient cultures besides just the Egyptians. For example, the Aryans in northeastern Iran (a region not far from where Gobekli Tepe is located) are known to have observed a 360-day year in ancient times that was also measured from around the time of the summer solstice. This calendar, which is referred to as the Old Avestan calendar, is thought to have had great similarity to both the oldest known Vedic calendar and, in some respects, to the post-Vedic calendar in India. A reference from the ancient *Yasht* text reported, "The year comes to an end . . . when the Tishtrya [Sirius] is in the rising." In Iran, the heliacal rising of Sirius was also seen as a predictor of coming rain, which was likewise seen as a boon to agriculture in that region.[10]

12

Ancestors, Dual Arms, and the Concept of the Embrace

Among the interesting enigmas we find at Gobekli Tepe are the anthropomorphized megalithic pillars, which include various human features, such as long arms with hands and stylized belts, that are carved in relief. Pillars with these features are surmised to have represented ancestors, a term that is associated in our cosmology with ancient teachers and a word that has cosmological significance in each of the ancient cultures we are studying. In his dictionary, Budge lists two words, *akeru* and *akriu,* that refer, respectively, to earth gods who were defined as ancestors and to a group of earth goddesses, the same term that defines the earth-goddess Tana Penu in the Sakti tradition.[1]

The prefix *ak* is one that we have discussed previously in association with the Egyptian word *akh,* meaning "light." In the Turkish language it refers to the color white, the color that Snodgrass associates with the full spectrum of light and that symbolizes creator-deities in our cosmology. We have already mentioned that *ak* is the phonetic root of the Turkish word *akbaba,* which means "vulture," a bird of prey that we associate with Gobekli Tepe, with our Sakta goddesses, with Isis and Nephthys in Egypt, and with the stars of Sirius. It also forms the root of the Turkish word *akrep,* meaning "scorpion," another creature that we associate with Gobekli Tepe and that is depicted in carvings there. It is the prefix of the Turkish word *akyildiz,* which refers to the Dog Star, Sirius. Clearly both the phoneme *ak/akh* and the related concept of ancestors stand as important connecting links between the cosmological traditions we have been pursuing and the sanctuary at Gobekli Tepe.

Budge also defines Asar, which is the name of the Egyptian god Osiris, as "the great Ancestor-god" of Egypt. In his dictionary entry, Budge recounts the myth of the dismemberment of Osiris, the classic Egyptian storyline that we noted in chapter 8 is told similarly in the Sakti tradition, but given there in relation to an archaic goddess rather than a god. Symbolically the name of Osiris is written with the Egyptian throne glyph and the eye glyph. We know that the throne, which is a traditional icon of the Egyptian goddess Isis, was also an archaic symbol of our Sakta earth goddess.

Figure 12.1. Name of Egyptian god Asar
(see Budge, *Egyptian Hieroglyphic Dictionary,* 83a)

Budge defines another term for "ancestor" that he pronounces *tepi a.*[2] We know, given the dozen meanings we have been able to correlate based on the Turkish word *tepe* and Egyptian *tep/tepi* words, that there could be associations between this term and the concept of an ancestor at Gobekli Tepe.

Budge defines yet another word for "ancestors" that he pronounces *ha-t.*[3] Spellings for this word center on a glyph that is the figure of the head and paws of a lion, comparable to the image of the Sphinx at Giza. The Sphinx is traditionally thought to have been carved from a natural outcropping of rock, and Brighenti tells us that in archaic times, such carvings were a characteristic of the Sakti tradition.

My first impulse when looking at the carved arms at Gobekli Tepe was that they might have been meant to convey the concept of dualism, similar to Budge's interpreted meaning for the dual-arm glyph, ◖◗, which Budge pronounces *ka*. From a cosmological standpoint this interpretation seems sensible, since dualism is defined as a principle of creation. However, several other concepts that we have explored in relation to Gobekli Tepe suggest the likelihood of another interpretation.

Perhaps the first overt clue to this interpretation is provided by an Egyptian word *skhen-t,* which means "pillar, support."[4] The pillar is cited by Brighenti as having symbolized the earth mother Tana Penu, and so calls to mind both the Sakta goddesses and the Gobekli Tepe structures. We relate this term phonetically to the Egyptian word *skhen,* meaning "to fold in the arms, to embrace, to contain, to hold."[5] Symbolically this word reads "to bind with the source of waves," followed by the image of a clay pot that is situated between dual arms. The clay pot image, in combination with an image of waves, suggests a possible association with a potbelly, a clay pot filled with water that also represented the Sakta earth goddess. Additionally, the notion of a pillar calls to mind a mythical theme of creation that is expressed by many ancient traditions in which the Earth was said to have been separated from the sky by the placement of four pillars at the cardinal points of east, west, north, and south. This theme seems to be reflected in an Egyptian word *skhenut,* which Budge says refers to "the four pillars of the sky."[6]

The ancestral mother figure who weaves matter in the Dogon tradition is a spider named Nana. Her name in the Egyptian hieroglyphic language means "to welcome, to salute joyfully," and it is expressed symbolically by a figure who stands with two outstretched arms, as if to invite a warm embrace. A second meaning of the Dogon word *nana* is "to wave the hand." As is appropriate to the role of the Dogon spider who weaves particles of matter from waves, this figure is shown holding a wave glyph on the palm of each hand.[7] The Dogon term that would be comparable to the concept of an "embrace" means "to move closer together," and it is expressed by the word *pene*.[8] This phonetic value suggests a possible relationship to the archaic term *penu* and to the Sakta goddess Tana Penu. From that perspective, the name of the goddess might be interpreted to mean "earth mother who embraces."

We also see concepts relating to an embrace reflected in the phonetic root *tem,* which we previously associated with various symbolic elements of Gobekli Tepe. Budge defines a word *tem* that means "to touch, approach, to come near to, to join, to be united, to bring together."[9] Through this meaning of the word *tem,* each of those other elements comes to be associated with the concept. Tem was also the name of an Egyptian earth god, and so relates conceptually to the earth goddesses of our Sakti tradition.

Because the Egyptian word for shrew mouse is *penu* and Ganesha was traditionally pictured alongside a rat, mouse, or shrew mouse, we would expect to find any symbolism that applies to the archaic term *penu* also reflected in relation to one or both of these concepts. As it turns out, there is an ancient tradition from Japan and China that explicitly associates Ganesha with the concept of an embrace. There Ganesha was sometimes pictured in a dual form called the Embracing Kangi, depicted as two tall figures with elephant heads, one male and one female, who stand closely together in a warm embrace. Other terms that are given to these embracing figures of Ganesha are Shoten or Shoden, Vinayaka, and, as previously mentioned, Kangi or Kangiten. These representations are thought by some researchers to have been of considerable importance in the traditional worship of Ganesha.[10]

In her book *Ganesa: A Monograph on the Elephant-Faced God,* Alice Getty explains the symbolism of the embracing Ganeshas as it was understood in China. Her belief is that the tradition originated in India and was brought from there into China and then carried to Japan. She associates it with the tantric tradition and specifically with

© 2013 Sylvie Kantorowitz

Figure 12.2. Two highly stylized versions of the Embracing Kangi, both showing the motherly embrace of the Sakti tradition. Left: in brass. Right: a modern depiction from children's illustrator Sylvie Kantorowitz.

the Orissa region as a tantric center. In all cases the doctrine was considered to be highly secretive, and in 1017 CE it was banned from inclusion in four volumes on the worship of Ganesha by the Chinese Emperor Chen Tsung. Getty says that while there are no known surviving historical images of the double form of Ganesha in China (likely because of the secrecy reflected by this edict), it's clear that a secret cult based on the idea was practiced there as late as the eleventh century CE. The tradition was linked with diagrams of a double mandala, which, in Getty's understanding, represented "the two sides of an Absolute Reality." She writes, "According to the esoteric explanation of the diagrams, the Garbha-dhatu represented the material, the phenomenal world, and the Vajra-dhatu, the spiritual, the noumenal world; and although they were apparently separate, they were in reality One and the Same or the Dharma-dhatu, that is, the Universe, the Cosmic world."[11]

Getty says that the secret existence of the two parts of the cosmos was taught to a disciple only after his or her official initiation into the tradition. We can conclude that it is for this reason that the image of the embracing Ganeshas, which we are aware of through surviving references in Japan and China, was steadfastly maintained as such a closely held secret.

Some researchers speak of Ganesha as a mediator between the material and divine worlds.[12] In that regard, there are a couple of points of interest to be noted about the image of the embracing Ganeshas. First, one is depicted wearing a hemispheric skullcap comparable to a *kepah* in Judaism, the hemispheric figure that we associate in our cosmology with mass, matter, and substance. The Ganesha with the kepah is also shown with a circular sun-glyph shape on his forehead, perhaps symbolic of our sun and our material universe. These details suggest that the two figures could also be symbolic of the material and nonmaterial universes, respectively.

Detailed specifications for how to make a statue of the dual Ganesha figures survived with the Shingon cult in Japan. They specify, "The image should be executed in metal and never higher than 22 inches. The two standing figures should be represented facing each other with the elephant-head posed on the left shoulder of the opposite figure and the arms of each encircling the other. They should wear long robes falling to the feet."[13]

It is also noteworthy that the overall impression given by the figure of the embracing Ganeshas bears outward similarities to the Dogon drawing of the nummo fish. This is an image that we interpret (based on statements made by the Dogon priests to Marcel Griaule) to symbolize the process by which matter (or "material") forms from nonmaterial waves. Supportive of this outlook, Getty says that in the most esoteric understanding of the dual Ganesha form, the two were conceptually fused into one.[14]

There are two enigmatic glyphs that appear on the Gobekli Tepe pillars that may well have bearing on this same concept of nonmaterial and material universes. The first takes the form of the letter H in the English alphabet, and the second again seems to be a representation of the Egyptian sun glyph—a circle with a central dot. (In truth, the H shape is given twice, once along the belt line of one of the "ancestor" pillars and once at the top front edge of a pillar. The H at the top of the Gobekli Tepe pillar may have actually been formed from a raised square with a central dot indented, similar to the central dot of an Egyptian sun glyph.) Because there are other contexts in which the sun glyph apparently denotes our material universe (such as that just mentioned in relation to the embracing Ganeshas and the symbolic representation of Sirius meeting the sun at the heliacal rising that defines the Dogon and Egyptian New Year, as discussed in the previous chapter), the suggestion is that these glyphs may have also been intended to symbolize the nonmaterial and material universes. From this perspective, these universes can also be seen to symbolize female and male principles, respectively. Support for this view is found with a little-known Masonic stonework symbol that is also drawn to look like an H and is understood to represent the joining of a female principle and a male principle. The concept of the symbol is explained in a 1913 article by J. W. Norwood called "Symbols and Science," published in a Masonic magazine called *The New Age Magazine*.

> The principle which brings about the union of energy and matter
> is an active, intelligent principle and thus formulated by one of the

Masters of Natural Science in the "Great Work": "There is a principle in nature which impels every entity to seek vibratory correspondence with a like energy of opposite polarity." This is the Law of Polarity, anciently called the Law of Motion and Number, the Law of Vibration, etc. Being an active principle and acting intelligently or by design (mathematical, if you will) and energy or force being the active factor in "creation" and generation, it is evident that "intelligence" is inherent in energy, not matter, and therefore that "Intelligence" is positive to matter. . . . Here then is matter and intelligence attracting each other. They unite. Here are two parallel lines. They unite because they attract each other. They are the ancient Father principle, positive male creative strength or energy, and the Mother principle, negative female productive energy. Join them where they touch our circle of inquiry and you have a third quantity—the created thing, indicated by a line. . . . The two joined lines tangent to the circle present us now the ancient "Mason's Mark" that looked so much like the letter H.[15]

In light of these widely varying references, the suggestion is that the dual arms pictured on the Gobekli Tepe pillars were meant to convey the concept of an embrace between the nonmaterial and material universes. An embrace would constitute the tangible act of "grasping and holding firm" that we associate symbolically with creator-deities in our tradition. The same concept could also relate to the admittedly less-huggable grasping action of the claws of birds of prey such as vultures, birds that also associate symbolically with the earliest creator-deities.

Budge defines a word *aa-t,* meaning "she who embraces," which can be looked at from this viewpoint.[16] Based on our interpretive outlook, this word reads "that which comes to earth" and defines the dual arms glyph: ⬭.

We know that the Egyptian concept of an embrace is one that relates symbolically to the processes of matter and more specifically

Figure 12.3. Egyptian word *aa-t,*
which means "she who embraces"
(see Budge, *Egyptian Hieroglyphic Dictionary,* 15b)

to Dogon concepts of the universe and the egg of the world, which is said to "wrap around" or "enclose" seeds of matter. Budge lists a word *anh,* which means "to surround, to enclose, to embrace, to wrap around." Symbolically, the glyphs of this word read "that by which the fish weaves the universe and the egg-of-the-world," followed by the particle glyph 𓋴𓈖. A second word, *anq,* means "to embrace, to gather together, to gird round." Symbolically it reads "that by which the fish weaves mass."[17]

Figure 12.4. Egyptian word *anh,* which means
"to surround, to enclose, to embrace, to wrap around"
(see Budge, *Egyptian Hieroglyphic Dictionary,* 63a)

A perhaps even more suggestive Egyptian word means "to open the arms" or "to embrace someone" and is pronounced *pega.* This word is written with the archaic shrine glyph and includes the image of two arms that enclose a pillar-like rectangle. Symbolically the word reads "the space of the temple, an embrace given as a sign or token." Budge defines the same word to represent the act of "unrolling papyrii,"[18] which is the concept that ultimately defines an ancient scroll such as a Jewish Torah.

There is an additional, somewhat more complex Egyptian word for "embrace" that begins with the very same glyphs that are used to write the word *meh,* meaning "cubit." We recall that the cubit is an archaic unit of measure common to many of the traditions we are studying that takes its definition from a person's arm and hand—the same two body parts depicted in relief on the Gobekli Tepe pillars. The term is pronounced *meh qena,* and symbolically it reads "the cubit: earth measure as an embrace."[19] A similar Egyptian word *meh* means "to seize, to have as a possession," and so again reflects the concept of "grasping."[20]

Another Egyptian word, *hapt,* meaning "to embrace," seems to symbolically link the concept to a sense of kindredness between the twin universes. One particular spelling that Budge relates to this word is written with the twisted rope glyph, which in our view resembles the figure of Amma's universes. The word also defines the dual arms. Symbolically, this word reads "two universes (non-material and material) embrace."[21]

Figure 12.5. Egyptian word *hapt,* which means "to embrace"
(see Budge, *Egyptian Hieroglyphic Dictionary,* 463a)

The same concept seems to be expressed symbolically by the Egyptian word *hept,* which means "to embrace, to hug, to take to the breast" and depicts the concept symbolically as the nonmaterial and material universes between two hugging arms.[22]

Figure 12.6. Egyptian word *hept,* which means
"to embrace, to hug, to take to the breast"
(see Budge, *Egyptian Hieroglyphic Dictionary,* 479a)

There is another set of interesting Egyptian words meaning "embrace, hug" that are based on the term *qena* and whose symbolic meanings seem to relate directly to our Sakta earth goddess and the feminine energy that relates to the Sakti tradition. This word for "embrace" is a homonym for the word *qena* that refers to a "bearing pole, litter, portable shrine." The meaning of "portable shrine" is also of particular interest to us in relation to this discussion because, due to their esoteric nature and the need for secrecy, figures of the Embracing Kangi were traditionally housed in portable shrines. The notion of a portable shrine calls to mind the Mongolian yurt, a kind of mobile stupa that I devoted a chapter of discussion to in *China's Cosmological Prehistory*.

The "bearing pole" definition is also of interest since we know that the pole was an archaic symbol of the Sakta goddesses. These words are based on a phonetic root, *qen,* that means "to be strong, to make strong, to fortify, to have power over, to overcome, to conquer, to be master of," which from the perspective of feminine energy seems comparable to our modern notion of a queen.[23]

Together, these words and symbols would seem to associate the concept of an embrace (or hug), which some would consider to be the warmest, most welcoming, sincere, and personal of gestures, with quite a number of the central themes of our creation plan. Through Egyptian word forms, the term "embrace" is given in relation to the earth goddess who represents an impressive mother figure of the tradition. An embrace is an action conducted in the human domain that effectively conveys the notion of grasping and holding firm, a phrase that is a hallmark of creator-deities in our cosmologies, such as Amma and Amen. In the Egyptian hieroglyphic dictionary, we find the definition of an embrace given in relation to phonetic roots that refer to ancestors, the ancient teachers who are credited with having brought instructed civilizing skills to humanity. We also see the concept of an embrace depicted prominently at Gobekli Tepe on megalithic pillars that are believed to symbolize those same ancestors. It is given in words that relate symbolically to the ritual shrine that serves as the grand symbol of the cosmology. We see it defined in terms of the cubit, the quintessential unit of measure used by initiates of the tradition to orient the aligned ritual shrine. And we see the symbolism of an embrace reflected in definitions of the Dogon egg of the world in the microcosm and of Barnard's Loop in the macrocosm, thereby linked by association to the signature phrase of the cosmology, "as above, so below.

13

Defining a Temple

The concept of a temple or sanctuary is one that we have touched on in this study from several different perspectives. We discussed the notion of a shrine in relation to an archaic Egyptian shrine glyph pronounced *het*. We talked about aligned ritual structures such as the Buddhist stupa and the Dogon granary and the role they play as grand mnemonic symbols of the cosmologies we are studying. We discussed archaic sanctuary names that appear to have been given in terms of the names of three deities or astronomical bodies. We noted apparent associations between these sanctuaries and certain temples of ancient Egypt. We talked about the very ancient megalithic sanctuary at Gobekli Tepe and the various symbolic elements that seem to be presented there. We talked about the archaic Sakti cult and the relationship of its goddesses to the stars of Sirius, mountaintop sanctuaries, carved outcroppings, three-stone cairns, circles of stone pillars with carved images of animals, and images of ancestors anthropomorphized with dual arms. We also discussed the Giza plateau, with its sanctuary-like structures that include the Sphinx, which is thought to have pointed to the heliacal rising of Sirius in archaic times. We know that a number of the animals pictured on the Gobekli Tepe megaliths, such as the vulture, the serpent, and the scorpion, were traditionally associated with the first kings and emperors of the ancient cultures we are studying. We can see from all of this that the concept of a temple touches on a wide range of symbolic elements that seem to relate in pivotal ways to the cosmologies we are studying.

There are also certain figures carved on the megaliths at Gobekli Tepe that do not represent animals. For instance, there is an image that takes the same general form as three side-by-side padlock-like figures, each carved with hemispheric shapes at the top and squared shapes below. Our exploration of archaic Egyptian glyphs and words suggests that these shapes may be representative of a glyph that Budge pronounces *het* and identifies with the term *temples*.[1] Budge documents a spelling for this word that is given as a single glyph, one that likewise presents three hemispheres or domes paired "above" with three squares "below" (symbolic of heaven and earth, from one perspective) all encapsulated within a rectangular border. Budge, apparently thinking that he is interpreting a modernized glyph rather than an archaic form, seemingly misinterprets the three repeating shapes as a classic Egyptian determinative for a plural form. Based on this outlook, he assigns the figure a meaning of "temples," whereas, based on other evidence, we interpret the glyph to be archaic and to reflect the singular cosmological definition of "a temple."

Support for this interpretation begins with a footnote written by Samuel Johnson in his work *Oriental Religions and Their Relation to Universal Religion*. His footnote is given as part of a discussion of an archaic type of Buddhist temple called a *chaitya*. He notes, "Three hemispheres . . . constitute the chaityas, or relic-temples, of the triple form of deity, Buddha, the Law and the Church."[2] This observation by Johnson is made from a nineteenth-century perspective and is cast phonetically in terms of the same complex *ch* phoneme as the archaic word for temple that Budge pronounces *get* and that we interpret as *het*.

It seems likely, based on our discussion of archaic temple names and Johnson's footnote, that from one perspective the archaic concept of a temple was intimately intertwined with the notion of three deities and from a cosmological perspective with three astronomical bodies symbolized by those deities. In two cases, regarding the sanctuary names Het

Penu Sa Ast, and Het Sa Ar Yah, I have argued that the archaic temple names referred to the two binary stars of Sirius, the three belt stars of Orion, and the spiral of Barnard's Loop. These are the same astronomical bodies that align symbolically with the three Buddhist stages of ascension described by Adrian Snodgrass, which he defines in relation to the images of three hemispheric domes. Sirius, the belt stars of Orion, and Barnard's Loop are also the three astronomical bodies that seem to overtly correspond to Snodgrass's step-by-step instructions, given from an earthbound perspective, for how to locate what he describes as a sun door or sun gate that is thought to exist between the Brahmanic and material universes.

Additional support for associating domes with the concept of a temple or sanctuary comes out of Iran. It is given in relation to the definition of a class of temple or sanctuary called a *gonbad,* where the dome is interpreted to represent a point of transition between the deity and mankind. One source states, "The sanctuary . . . is the place where God and Mankind meet and can converse. The natural symbol for this is the Universe . . . [which encloses] mankind in a protective space. . . . The Dome is thus a shape of great symbolic importance which must be replicated through the properties of matter. . . . The dome thus becomes a symbol of the cosmic house of God which in turn has the dual meaning of the House that God inhabits—Heaven, and the house that encompasses Man—the Universe. The dome acts therefore as a transition between the infinite . . . and mankind."[3]

Snodgrass also discusses the symbolism of the dome in his work *Architecture, Time, and Eternity.* Here he says, "The dome and its supporting base symbolize the union of the complementary principles of Essence and Substance, symbolically identified with the dome of the heavens and the cube of the earth . . . the marriage of the dome and its base is the union of time and space."[4]

There is an Egyptian term for "sanctuary" that Budge gives as *hephep* and defines as "the name of a sanctuary."[5] This word is based on a phonetic root *hep,* reminiscent of our archaic term for a temple, *het.* Budge defines the word *hep* to mean "turn, turning, solstice, dual, southern solstice, northern solstice, the limits or ends of the earth."[6] Budge gives one spelling for this word that is based on the same twisted rope glyph, 𐤀, that we associate with the Dogon drawing of Amma's heliacal universe, and the square glyph, □, and hemisphere glyph, ⌒, that we take in this context to symbolize the nonmaterial and material universes. Another spelling of the word *hep* is written with three sun-like rayed hemispheres that are perhaps symbolic of the solstices and the equinox. The two annual equinoxes and the intermediate solstice are the same three positions of the sun that define the movements of the east-west oriented line of the base plan of a Buddhist stupa. So from this additional perspective, we could also reasonably associate the concept of a shrine or temple with three hemispheres. Support for this solar-linked viewpoint is found in a second Egyptian word, *hephep,* which Budge says refers to a "God of the ecliptic."[7] The term *ecliptic* is the name for a circular line in astronomy that defines the apparent motions of the sun.

The Dogon drawing of the fourteen paired universes created by Amma depicts the universes in the form of alternating squares and circles, and so the notion of "squaring the circle" can be taken in this context as a metaphor for reconciling the two universes. The hemisphere is a geometric figure that actually combines those two shapes, and so can be seen to be symbolic of their union. So we can see that there are a number of distinct perspectives from which the shape of a hemisphere—often three hemispheres—reasonably associates with the concept of a temple. It is my contention that these hemispheres, symbolic of the archaic notion of a temple or sanctuary, are the same essential figures that we find inscribed on the megalithic pillars at Gobekli Tepe.

The definition of ascension that Snodgrass describes in terms of his diagram of three hemispheres (see page 93) also provides a rationale for the archaic form of the three-stone cairns that represented the Sakta goddesses from ancient times. From that viewpoint, each stone would symbolize one of the hemispheres. As I noted in chapter 7, Marcel Griaule includes a photograph in *The Pale Fox* of a three-stone Dogon cairn that is similarly configured, complete with a flat topping stone.[8] A cairn arguably defines the same essential symbolism as a Buddhist stupa, whose geometric form serves to mark out the three stations of the sun at its times of the solstice and the two equinoxes.

We can relate the cairn form more specifically to the concept of an archaic mountaintop sanctuary based on a Turkish word *huyuk,* a word that means "cairn" and may be familiar from the name of yet another well-known archaic sanctuary in Turkey called Çatalhüyük. This correlation derives from another Turkish phrase, *tepe biciminde mezar,* which also means "cairn" or, literally, "grave in the form of a hill or mountain," a meaning that effectively defines the concept of sky burial, a ritual practice that researchers tentatively associate with the structures at Gobekli Tepe.

14

The Bridge of Sirah

Applied symbolique can be compared to the Bridge of Sirah in the Islamic Qur'an. It is as wide as a razor's edge; on either side is a yawning gulf of perdition. One precipice is the mentality of logical or mathematical reason, the other is superstition.

R. A. Schwaller de Lubicz

The metaphoric image quoted above is taken from a book called *The Egyptian Miracle: An Introduction to the Wisdom of the Temple,* by symbolist R. A. Schwaller de Lubicz.[1] It refers to an esoteric Islamic tradition called Surah Baqarah, which describes the processes by which the universe was said to have been created, as they are given in the Qu'ran. These descriptions tell of seven interrelated firmaments of the galactic system that are understood to have emerged concurrently with one another, within a single framework of space and time. By comparison to Dogon definitions, these firmaments would correspond conceptually to the seven material universes created by Amma, and so can be thought of as representing the substantive half of the fourteen paired Dogon universes.[2]

From a phonetic standpoint, the word *surah,* or *sirah,* can be understood in the same way as other key terms of our plan of cosmology, as a compound of two conceptual phonemes. Time and again we have seen the phonetic value *si* associated with the stars of Sirius, most obviously in the name Sirius itself. We also see it in the name of the Egyptian goddess Isis and in the name of the archaic Indian deity Siva. We even see a possible phonetic relationship to the "si" of Sirius in the name of the Egyptian god Osiris, symbolic of Orion, whose belt stars the Dogon consider to be "deputies" of Sirius. In the Turkish language, the word *sira* refers to an "ordered sequence," "progression," or "lineage." The word is formed from a phonetic root *sir,* which means "secret."

Genevieve Calame-Griaule tells us that the Dogon word *si* means "family or category" and refers to four categories of principles that relate to the four primordial elements.[3] The Dogon term *si:re* means "to extend or spread out in front of oneself."[4] This same phonetic value *si* is reflected in the Dogon name for Sirius, *sigi tolo,* and in the name of the Dogon Sigi festival of Sirius. We likely see a variation on the phoneme in the correlating Egyptian term *skhai,* meaning "to celebrate a festival."

The term *ra,* which we interpret as the second of the compound phonemes of *sirah,* is a familiar name in our cosmologies for the sun and in the context of galactic symbolism stands for the universe of our sun. The Dogon and Buddhists associate our material universe with a womb, and that meaning is reflected in a Turkish word for "womb," *rahim.*

Speaking from the perspective of ancient Egyptian symbolism, Schwaller de Lubicz suggests in his statement that, regardless of which outlook we may entertain regarding concepts of creation, be it primarily a scientific or spiritual one, any search for truth within these ancient mystery traditions may require us to stretch the limits of our own personal philosophy and ask us to allow for possibilities that could extend beyond the expectations of our own familiar worldview. Schwaller de Lubicz's belief is that answers to the most fundamental questions of creation will ultimately be discovered to lie somewhere in between where a traditional scientist and a strict spiritualist might expect to find them.

There is an ancient esoteric form of Judaism called Kabbalism that addresses many of these same fundamental questions of creation. They are expressed in a philosophy similar to the Islamic Bridge of Sirah tradition, referred to in Kabbalism as the doctrine of N'Sirah or Nisera. The Kabbalah defines two modes of divine energy: one that is "straight, linear, or erect" and is considered to be "masculine," and one that is "round or curved" and is seen as "feminine." These definitions correlate well with the symbolism of the square and the circle as they are understood within our cosmology, where the figure of the square defines the concept of "earth" and associates with a male creator-god such as Fu-xi in China, and the circle symbolically defines "heaven" and may relate to a female mother goddess such as China's Nu-wa. But within this context, the symbolic assignments of circle and square are made on a cosmic level to the nonmaterial and material universes, rather than to the more earth-oriented concepts of "heaven and earth." However, the focus of this galactic symbolism can be seen once again to center on the notion of reconciling a square with a circle.

In the Kabbalist tradition of N'Sirah, the female energy is understood to surround and enfold the male energy, and so reflects the same essential concept of an embrace that we have seen symbolized in so many other aspects of our cosmology. However in this case the symbolism plays out in relation to a kind of "hugging" relationship that is supposed to exist between the pairs of nonmaterial and material universes.[5] The same concept is reflected in the dual nature of the Dogon creator-god Amma, whose name means "to hold firmly, to embrace strongly."[6]

The alternating upward/downward motion that characterizes the creation of these universes in the Dogon and Buddhist traditions is conveyed for the Kabbalists during an annual ritual of Judaism that is observed during the High Holy Days, which are celebrated around the time of the New Year. It is expressed through the metaphoric waving of the branches of four species of plants. These include the willow, palm, and myrtle, which are bound together and referred to collectively as the *lulav,* and a fourth plant, the citron, which is referred to as the *etrog.* The ritual waving or shaking of these plants symbolizes "vibration or movement" in six directions, comparable to the six spatial directions that define the axis of the Dogon egg of the world. The individual who performs these motions is understood to represent the conceptual center point of that circle and so constitutes a "seventh direction." Although the numerology of the N'Sirah tradition plays out somewhat differently than it does for the Dogon tradition, these motions end up defining a series of paired universes that are comparable to the universes of Amma and are defined as being alternately spiritual and material in character. The Kabbalist symbolism is given in relation to a *sukkah,* a traditional hut built from branches and twigs that serves as a kind of conceptual gateway to a higher dimension. (A similar Egyptian term, *skhet,* means "to erect a shelter made of leaves and branches."[7]) This higher dimension relates to a feminine mode of divinity comparable to the feminine energy that is associated with the mother goddesses of the Sakti tradition.[8]

Snodgrass tells us that in India, Brahmanic formulations of symbolism as they relate to creation are given in terms of an "essential" male principle of manifestation called *purusa* and a "substantial" female principle that is laid down prior to all other things, called *praktri.* In mythology, these are personified as the male creator-god Siva and the mother goddess Sakti, or Sati,[9] the archaic male and female creator-deities of our Sakti cult in Orissa.

From this perspective in Buddhism, the domains of the nonmaterial and material universes are alternately conceptualized in relation to three component aspects of a dome or hemisphere: the circular dome itself represents the nonmaterial universe and is defined by the symbolic term "heaven," the flat base of the dome represents our material universe, called "earth," and the area above the base that is enclosed within the structure of the dome is referred to as "midspace." The dome itself is defined conceptually as the "upper waters," and its base is conceptualized as resting on the "lower waters."[10] The suggestion is that, like the natural water cycle of our planet, the upward/downward circulation of these "waters" is essential to life within our cosmic domain of existence.

Within the context of these definitions we find virtually all of the essential symbolic elements of the cosmologies we have been pursuing. Among them we have a female principle that manifests a male principle, who respectively are defined as "heaven and earth" and are characterized as "above and below." They are given in symbolic relationship to the geometric figures of a circle and a square. Based on this symbolism, any attempt to rationally integrate the relationship of these two universes with the underlying processes of creation is compared metaphorically to the act of reconciling a square with a circle. Within these definitions we also have a view of creation that manifests itself from water, is fundamentally rooted in vibration, is founded on a principle of duality, and begins at the center of a circle and emanates outward in seven directions. These descriptions define galactic creation in terms of seven material universes that are functional counterparts to the seven dimensions of the Dogon egg of the world.

One central idea relative to the creation of the universe that is shared commonly by various traditions we are studying is the tenet that a second nonmaterial universe formed side by side with our material one, as its conceptual twin. This same outlook is expressed in the Vedic tradition in conjunction with the belief that the two universes are destined to someday reverse themselves. Belief in the notion of an eventual reversal between the universes is also expressed in other traditions, such as the Dogon and Kabbalism.

The Dogon priests describe an inherent structural difference between the two types of universes that centers on the timing of how and when membranes appear during the formation of matter. They view this difference as a fundamental flaw in our material universe, one that resulted when one of the later stages of creation took place out of its proper sequence. The Kabbalists also consider our material universe to be inherently flawed, but express the idea metaphorically as myth rather than through overt cosmology. They represent it in terms of the symbolic union of two ancestral beings, Adam and Eve, and the familiar Christian notion of an original sin. Like the formation of the Dogon membranes of matter, the primordial joining of Adam and Eve is also said to have happened prematurely, or before the appointed time. For reasons that are dismissed as "too complicated to explain," Adam and Eve chose to consummate their relationship on the final day of Sukkot rather than waiting until the proscribed evening of the following Shabbat. This transgression, expressed here through mythic storyline, resulted in an inherent flaw in our universe.

The Kabbalists contend that the ultimate remedy to this flaw lies with the ritual observance of the High Holy Days of Judaism, ten days that are observed annually in conjunction with the New Year, which the Kabbalists say symbolize the progressive stages of creation. Because this remedy must now be carried out in the "real time" of the human sphere, as compared to what is described as the accelerated time frame of the original creation, tradition holds that this remedy will only accomplish its effect after an extended period of approximately six thousand years. It may be worth noting that, as I write these words, the current Hebrew year is counted as 5774.

The general contours of the theme of N'Sirah are evident in the traditions of ancient China, where the opposing but complementary notions of yin and yang are defined symbolically as representing earth and heaven, respectively. Snodgrass defines them as "metaphysical principles that are 'reflected' into phenomena," in much the same way that our material world "reflects" an underlying reality for the Dogon.[11] Snodgrass tells us that the notion of yang relates to concepts of essence, while yin corresponds to the notion of substance. Just as the Dogon compare the dynamic relationship between the paired universes to the recurring stages of the natural water cycle, so Snodgrass tells us that the conditions of yin and yang are each understood to "proceed" from the essential nature of the other. The Chinese terms *yin* and *yang* might also be compared to two Dogon principles called *ana* and *ya,* where ana represents the male principle of creation and ya represents the female.

Finally, the idea of two paired universes conceptualized as twins, which provides the conceptual foundation for the doctrine of N'Sirah, has possible bearing on our previous discussion of the embracing Ganeshas, who are also symbolic of the two universes. The key to what may have been intended by the term *twins* comes from yet another word entry in Budge's dictionary that means "to be twins" or "to be friends." This word is pronounced *heter,* and so is based on the same phonetic root that we associate with temples or sanctuaries. The glyphs used to spell the word begin with the twisted rope glyph, which calls to mind the drawing of Amma's multiple universes, and include the hemisphere glyph, which is also the symbol of a womb that has been invoked previously to represent our material universe. The suffix *ter* calls to mind the Egyptian word *ter-ti,* which Budge defines as "two birds, i.e., Isis and Nephthys," who are symbolic of the twin stars of Sirius and the two Sakta goddesses. From our perspective, the word defines a trailing glyph that depicts two figures who stand hand in hand with one another. Like the embracing Ganeshas, the intent conveyed by both the word and the defined image seems to be a most sincere and welcoming one, expressive of warmth, friendship, and mutual support.

15

The Cosmological Role of Ganesha

The evolution of Ganesha as a god in India is one that, due to the lack of surviving evidence, has a long but sometimes unclear history. Although there are suggestive references to elephant worship as early as 200 BCE that some researchers interpret as referring to Ganesha, the earliest known iconic images of him date only from around the fifth century CE. Among the three oldest carved images, in two cases Ganesha is pictured with two arms, and in the third with four arms. Nonetheless, Ganesha, like the Sakti tradition with which he is intimately associated, is understood to be an exceedingly archaic form. In the introduction to Alice Getty's book *Ganesa: A Monograph on the Elephant-Faced God,* Alfred Foucher writes:

> Obviously Ganesa is linked with those stout, thick-set goblins with which the earliest sculptures of ancient India have made us familiar. . . . For sheer antiquity, their race can hold its own. These . . . spring up from a family which can be traced, since time began, from one end of the continent [of India] to the other. . . . One must be as short-sighted as a bookworm to deduce from the lack of any mention of Ganesa in the early epics, that the god did not exist before the fourth or fifth cen-

tury of our own era [or that] his worship [could have been] established throughout the whole of India at such a comparatively recent date.[1]

Our discussions have shown that there are several different cosmological perspectives from which Ganesha can be seen to symbolize Barnard's Loop, the spiraling birthplace of stars that centers on the belt stars of Orion. We argued in chapter 16 of *The Cosmological Origins of Myth and Symbol* that Barnard's Loop is the structure that is referenced by the Dogon concept of the chariot of Orion and is the mythical chariot wheel that is associated in many traditions with the grand precessional cycle of rotation of the stars. The Dogon say that our region of space is regulated by the hub of this wheel, and descriptions given from the Buddhist perspective by Snodgrass suggest that the binary stars of Sirius constitute that hub. Based on descriptions and diagrams given by Snodgrass, we also believe that the Buddhist concept of ascension in the macrocosm centers on the Orion belt stars, Barnard's Loop, and the Sirius stars.

We believe that these same three astronomical structures—Barnard's Loop, the belt stars of Orion, and the Sirius stars—are referenced in Budge's archaic sanctuary name Ga nu sa Ast (alternately, Het Penu Sa Ast). In Egypt, the term *penu* refers to a mouse, and the name Hetes to a shrew mouse deity, and so we take Ga nu sa as a likely reference to Ganesha, an archaic god in India and Asia who is overtly associated with a mouse. We know that Sa is an Egyptian name for Osiris/Orion and Ast a name for Isis/Sirius. From a cosmological perspective, it is Barnard's Loop that would associate with Orion and Sirius as a triad.

The word *penu* led us to the two archaic sister goddesses of the Sakti cult in Orissa, Dharni Penu and Tana Penu, who are linked mythically to Ganesha and are traditionally pictured in the company of Ganesha. These sisters were symbolized by a throne, the very same icon that defines Isis/Sirius in ancient Egypt. Dharni Penu, whose name means "luminous," is a good symbolic match for Isis and the sunlike star Sirius A, while the name of the earth mother Tana Penu combines

two cosmological phonemes, *ta* and *na*, that are symbolic of "earth/
mass" and "mother," and so present a good symbolic match for the massive dwarf star Sirius B.

Barnard's Loop is also the macrocosmic structure that the Dogon
priests correlate to the po pilu in the microcosm of matter. The po pilu
is the Dogon egg of the world that would compare to the Calabi-Yau
space of string theory. Astronomically, Barnard's Loop is an example of
a stellar bubble, the scientific definition of which is a very close match
for Dogon descriptions of the po pilu. For the Dogon, these structures
constitute a point of correlation between the processes of the macrocosm and the microcosm and the apparent link by which the phrase "as
above, so below" can be demonstrated.

Ancient myths in India define Ganesha as a white elephant and
(depending on which myth you believe) the son either of the god Siva
alone; of just Paravati/Sati, who was the consort of Siva; or of both Siva
and Paravati/Sati together (some myths say Ganesha had two mothers).
There is also a tradition that actually equates Ganesha with Siva based
on a commonly shared set of symbols and designations. In the myths
of Nepal, Siva and Paravati were not considered to be the parents of
Ganesha. Rather, it was said that Ganesha was self-created and became
visible of his own free will from a ray of sunshine or light.[2] The name
he was given there, Surya-Vinayaka, reflects that symbolism and a likely
relationship to Barnard's Loop, since Surya was the chief solar deity
in Hinduism and was depicted as riding on a chariot pulled by seven
horses (or alternately, by a single horse with seven heads).

We know that the Dravidian word *pilu* means "elephant," and it
can also mean "son"; in addition, the Dogon term *pilu* means "white."
We also know that the Sanskrit word *pil* means "elephant," as does the
Turkish word *fil*. The Dravidian word *pille* refers to the white "tusk"
of an elephant. Given these commonalities, our reasonable expectation
is that we should encounter cosmological symbolism for Ganesha that
would link him in positive ways to the Dogon concept of the po pilu.

As it turns out, this is precisely what we find in an ancient Indian text called the *Mudgala Purāna*. Phyllis Granoff of Yale University writes in an article entitled "Ganeśa as Metaphor: The *Mudgala Purāna*":

> The *Mudgala Purāna* in a way may be understood to frame its narratives with a discussion of creation; it first introduces the discussion of creation in book 1, chapter 6, and the last book repeats the description with slight variation, in 9:1. The topic in fact comes up again and again in the text, as if to underscore its importance. As is the case with many of the philosophical concepts in the text, creation is not only described directly in a dialogue that is taking place between various individuals. It is also described in hymns, in which Ganeśa is praised as a variety of entities that represent the various stages of the absolute as it unfolds in the world. These entities are listed in the order in which they appear in creation, and it thus becomes possible to reconstruct the process of creation from the hymn.[3]

The *Mudgala Purāna* defines eight incarnations of Ganesha in terms that can be seen as a close conceptual match for the Dogon egg of the world. At the most obvious level of interpretation, these relate to a diagram from Griaule and Dieterlen's *The Pale Fox* that outlines the stages of what they refer to as "development inside the seed." These stages are conceptualized as seven rays (or vibrations) of a star that are of increasing length. The complete figure with seven rays is characterized by the spiral that can be drawn to inscribe the endpoints of these rays. (Note that the seven stages of the drawing in figure 15.1 on page 140 progress from right to left and do not include the eighth conceptual stage, in which the seventh ray of the emerging star grows long enough to pierce the "egg.")

Granoff assigns the name Vakratunda, which means "twisting trunk," to the first incarnation of Ganesha. She says that this stage of creation is representative of "the absolute as the aggregate of all bodies,

Figure 15.1. Development inside the seed
(see Griaule and Dieterlen, *Pale Fox*, 137; also see the diagram
from Scranton, *Science of the Dogon*, 80)

an embodiment of the form of Brahman." In our view, the phrase "twisting trunk" offers an excellent description for the first (rightmost) stage of the Dogon po pilu, which actually looks like a twisting trunk. The purpose of this incarnation of Ganesha is to overcome the demon of envy or jealousy.

The Egyptian term for "absolute" is formulated from phonetic roots that mean "non-existent" or "empty of." One such Egyptian root is pronounced *ga*.[4] Granoff notes that the traditional *vahana*, or mount of Ganesha, at this incarnation is a lion. In Egypt, the image of a lion can symbolize the "first or foremost aspect" of a thing.[5]

Budge defines an Egyptian word for "the trunk of an elephant" that is pronounced *te-t*.[6] The same pronunciation refers to "part of a chariot," which Budge surmises may be a pole. However, the symbolic correlation we make between the po pilu and Barnard's Loop (which is defined in our cosmology as the wheel of a chariot) suggests that the reference may actually be to the wheel-like spiral.

This initial stage of twisting, associated with the creation of matter, recalls a concept I discussed in *China's Cosmological Prehistory*, which is referred to as "the pivot of the four quarters." The term refers to the complex way in which primordial waves are said to be raised up and twisted during the earliest stages of the formation of matter. From the perspective of Egyptian root words that survive in later languages, the term *absolute* could sensibly combine the prefix *ab* (on which the word for "elephant" is based) with the term *s-rut*, which means "to make to grow or flourish."[7]

The second incarnation of Ganesha is referred to by the name Ekadanta, which means "single tusk." This stage represents "the aggregate of all living souls, an embodiment of the essential nature of Brahman." The purpose of this incarnation is to overcome the demon of arrogance or conceit. Again, the phrase "single tusk" seems like a very good characterization of the second Dogon figure, which we can compare to the typical astronomical image of a supernova. (In the Dogon conception of creation, stages of creation of matter are linked conceptually to creational processes in the larger universe and often take the same forms.) The word Brahman is a term that we associate with the cosmological concept of the primeval waters, an idea that is expressed by the Dogon and Egyptian term *nu.* At this second incarnation, Granoff defines Ganesha's mount as a mouse.

The third incarnation of Ganesha is called Mahodara, meaning "big belly." It is considered to be the synthesis or conceptual offspring of the first two stages of Vakratunda and Ekadanta. It is "the absolute as it enters into the creative process" and is "an embodiment of the wisdom of Brahman." One Egyptian term for "belly" is *kha-t,* and it can be spelled using three uteruses or wombs, which we take as symbolic, both of the first three divisions of the "egg" and of the three rayed lines that characterize the third stage of the Dogon figure. The purpose of this incarnation is to overcome the demon of delusion or confusion. The likely equivalent Egyptian term is pronounced *sa* and means both "opener of the belly" and "son" or "firstborn son."[8] This word also represents the phonetic root of the Egyptian term Sati, a title for Isis and Nephthys, the Egyptian sister goddesses that we equate to our Sakta goddesses Tana Penu and Dharni Penu. A direct relationship between the Vedic goddess Sati and our Sakta goddesses is reflected in the motherly relationship they all share to Ganesha, who is cast in some myths as the son Sati created from clay, but also sometimes referred to as "he who has two mothers." At this incarnation, Ganesha's mount is defined as a mouse.

It seems significant that the likely Egyptian terms for these first three incarnations of Ganesha are expressed by the phonetic values *ga, nu,* and *sa,* and culminate in a reference to the opening of a belly (perhaps symbolic of a birth) and the notion of a firstborn son. As we have noted, in the Sakti tradition Ganesha was often characterized as the son of Sati. Likewise, the figures depicted in these stages call to mind Snodgrass's three aspects of ascension, in that they are given in terms of a spiral, a straight-line figure comparable to the line of an axis that is divided by a centerpoint, and a figure with three points. Moreover, these figures are actually said to depict the first three stages of the ascension of matter as it occurs in the microcosm. The corresponding macrocosmic stages of ascension relate to the three astronomical bodies whose names we interpreted to be Penu, Ast, and Sa, and to Budge's archaic sanctuary name, Ga nu sa Ast.

The fourth incarnation of Ganesha relates to the name Gajavaktra (or Gajanana), meaning "elephant face." The likely corresponding Egyptian term is *abu*, which means "elephant."[9] This word is formed on the phonetic root *ab*, which Budge defines as meaning "to face, meet, join or unite with someone or something." The word *ab* also refers to the "horn or tusk of an elephant" and to the "four horns of the world," a concept that implies the cosmological notion of the four cardinal points. The associated Dogon stage of the po pilu drawing depicts four rays of a star that resemble four horns and are configured like an axis that divides the egg of the world. Granoff tells us that the purpose of this incarnation of Ganesha is to overcome the demon of greed. Appropriate to that purpose, another Egyptian term *ab* means "to wish for, to desire, to long for."[10] Granoff says that at this incarnation, Ganesha's mount is defined as a mouse.

It is worthy of note that the Egyptian terms *ab*, meaning "to join or unite with," and *aab*, meaning "to wish for, to desire, to love," which are expressed with the same phonetic root as the Egyptian words *abu*, meaning "elephant," and *abu*, meaning "people, men and women,"[11] seem to reflect the same intention that underlies the concept of the embracing Ganeshas. We find these references at the fourth stage of the Dogon egg of the world, the point that would be the microcosmic counterpart to the fourth of Amma's seven material universes and that, according to the Dogon, defines our own universe. We might interpret this symbolism as another overt expression of the mutuality and friendship that characterizes Ganesha in the macrocosm. In the mundane world, the two universes (nonmaterial and material) that seem to be so warmly symbolized by the embracing Ganeshas are brought together in the form of the sanctuary or shrine, a concept that Budge defines with the term *ab-t*.[12]

The figure associated with the fourth incarnation of Ganesha again evokes the Chinese image of the "four quarters," the notion on which ancient Chinese concepts of land management and civic planning were based. In our view, this figure relates to the same set of concepts that underlie the ancient Chinese name Fu-xi, which we interpret to mean "celebrates the four." In *China's Cosmological Prehistory,* we argued, based on an alternate configuration of the shape, that it is the same essential figure that is depicted by the Egyptian town glyph, ⊗.

Granoff tells us the fifth incarnation of Ganesha corresponds to "the pure power of Brahman" that is defined by the term *sakti*. This term is central to the concept of ascension that we discussed in chapter 9 in relation to Snodgrass. The likely Egyptian correlate is the word *sakh,* which means "to raise up, to lift up on high."[13] Granoff says that the purpose of this incarnation is to overcome the demon of anger. This aspect of Ganesha is likely expressed by the Egyptian word *skhun,* which means "wrathful, angry. Furious."[14] Granoff's name for this incarnation is Lambodara, which means "pendulous belly" and could possibly relate to the Egyptian word *sa,* which means "slave of the belly."[15] At this incarnation, Ganesha's mount is again defined as a mouse.

The sixth incarnation of Ganesha is represented by the name Vikata, meaning "unusual form" or "misshapen." Granoff tells us that Vikata corresponds to Surya, who is traditionally seen as a sun deity. The same concept in Buddhist cosmology was represented by the entity known as Ri Gong Ri. In Egypt, the suggested counterpart would be Ra, whose cosmological symbolism we relate to the bending or warping ("misshaping") of mass by the force of gravity. Granoff says the purpose of this incarnation of Ganesha was to overcome the demon of lust. A comparable Egyptian term for "lust" is given by Budge as *rib*.[16] At this stage of creation, Ganesha's mount is understood to be a peacock. The peacock is an animal that, along with the mongoose, is often cast symbolically as an enemy of the serpent. Although Budge lists no Egyptian word in his dictionary for "peacock," the reference could be symbolic of the spectrum of colors that is symbolized by the peacock and could relate to the Egyptian term *ri-t,* which means "ink or colours of the scribe." Supportive of this viewpoint, Snodgrass defines a geometric Buddhist symbol that is comparable to a Jewish star (it combines two inverted triangles inscribed within a circle) in which each of the six star points relates to a color of the spectrum.[17]

The seventh incarnation of Ganesha is Vighnaraja, which means "king of obstacles" and corresponds to Vishnu. The purpose of this incarnation is to overcome the demon of possessiveness. The definition "king of obstacles" is a likely correlate to the Egyptian term *shenu,* which means "to encircle, surround, enclose or obstruct."[18] The notion of encircling, surrounding, or enclosing accurately defines the Dogon concept of the po pilu, and actions that involve obstruction are a traditional attribute of Ganesha. Another Egyptian word *shenu* refers to "a court official" or "the court of a king."[19] For the Dogon, the seventh stage of the po pilu represents its completion as the egg of the world, the fundamental unit on which all matter is based. Vishnu is similarly understood to represent the all-pervading essence of all beings and to be the master of the past, present, and future. As such, Vishnu, like the Dogon egg of the world, originates and develops all elements within the universe. Here Granoff tells us that Ganesha's mount is the celestial serpent Shesha—as we noted, the enemy of the peacock. From the perspective of our Dogon/Egyptian cosmology, the serpent symbolizes this same completed structure, which is characterized as the finished Word of matter. In concert with the Dogon meaning, Budge tells us that the Egyptian word *sheser* refers to the concept of "utterance, speech or decree."[20]

The eighth incarnation of Ganesha is called Dhumravarna, meaning "grey color," and corresponds to Siva, the consort of Sati in the Sakti tradition. He represents the destructive nature of Brahman. The purpose of this incarnation is to overcome the demon of pride. In Dogon cosmology, the eighth conceptual stage of the po pilu involves its destruction, an event that transpires when the seventh ray of the internal star grows long enough to finally pierce the egg. This event is also understood to initiate the formation of the next egg in the series, whose relationship to the first is compared to that of "pearls on a string." In Egypt, the notion of an implement of destruction that could facilitate the piercing of an egg is conveyed by a term formed from the phonetic root *ska,* meaning "an object like a short javelin," which could be descriptive of the seventh ray of the egg. The Egyptian word *skami* refers to the concept of "greyness," and the term *s-kam-kam* means "to destroy, to overthrow, to annihilate."[21] At this final stage of incarnation, Ganesha's mount is understood to be a mouse.

Granoff tells us that the cosmological import of Ganesha is conceptualized in two distinct ways: first given in the details (just described) of his eight incarnations, but then also given again in over-view. Taking one step back from the cosmology of matter to what we perceive more properly as a concept of biological creation, she explains that existence is also understood to arise in relation to the union of a female principle called *prakrti* and a male principle called *purusa.* The Dogon priests offer an alternate outlook on the seven-rayed egg figure that corresponds to Granoff's cosmology for Ganesha, as seen in figure 15.2 on page 146.

From this alternate perspective seen in figure 15.2, the seven rays are conceptualized as a kind of stick figure, which in Granoff's terms we can deem to represent Ganesha. In the figure on the right, the seventh and longest ray is depicted in two segments, to convey the idea of it piercing the egg. This same symbolism may well be what is expressed by an ancient myth that relates to Ganesha, in which his right tusk comes to be broken. Also in the figure on the right, the two upper rays are grouped together to signify a head, the next two lower rays represent

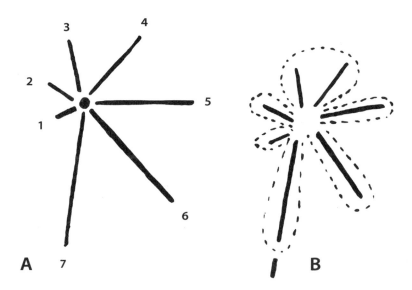

Figure 15.2. Seven vibrations inside the po pilu
(see Griaule and Dieterlen, *Pale Fox*, 139)

the arms, the following two lower rays symbolize legs, and the seventh ray represents the "sex" of the figure, or might alternately be seen as the single tusk that is sometimes associated with images of Ganesha. This symbolism is understood numerologically as grouping the four upper rays together to represent the female principle and the three lower rays to represent the male principle. Taken together in combination, these total seven, which for the Dogon is the number of the individual. Another way to conceptualize this drawing would be to consider the middle rays to be four arms and to posit, based on the unpaired seventh ray, that the figure, like some images of Ganesha, stands (or dances) on one foot. Looked at in this way, the figure effectively defines the two primary ways in which Ganesha is traditionally depicted in art: with two arms and a single tusk or with four arms and dancing.

We observed in *The Science of the Dogon* that this numerology could also have biological significance in relation to DNA, where the sex of an individual is determined by the presence of an X or a Y chromosome. The X chromosome (with four branches) establishes the biology of a female, while the Y chromosome, which has only three branches, establishes the biology of a male. Looked at from this perspective, we see an underlying rationale for conceptualizing two interlinked Ganeshas: one symbolically male, the other female.

Dogon definitions for the terms *ga, nu,* and *sa* offer some interesting perspectives on the complex traditional role Ganesha plays as the introducer and remover of obstacles. First, Genevieve Calame-Griaule defines the Dogon phoneme *ga* as a subordinate particle that expresses conditionality in several different ways. It can represent an expression of a desire to be satisfied, such as, "I would like to eat now." It can be used to express an obstacle to be overcome in a causative sense, such as, "Because I am sick, I will not be able to work." Or it can be used in relation to a difficulty in a restrictive sense, similar to the example, "Although the dog does not deserve to . . ." It also is used like the English word *but* to introduce a conceptual opposition.

The Dogon term *nu* relates to a concept that is pivotal both to the cosmology and to the rite of divination. It means "bean." Calame-Griaule explains that the Dogon mix their beans with sand to preserve them for later use, then later use a sieve to separate the beans from the sand and restore them to usability. In Dogon cosmology, the concept of a sieve is given as a metaphor for the processes of the po pilu, which function as an act of separation; they work to transform matter in its sandlike/wavelike form into bean-like particles. For beans, this separation is accomplished through the introduction of an obstacle that, from a conceptual standpoint, is productive and beneficial—the sieve. This same metaphor relates to Dogon divination, whose defined purpose is to separate truth from error.

The sieve is a concept we previously associated with the weaving of matter and the po pilu in *Sacred Symbols of the Dogon*. The symbolism relates to an Egyptian word that means "to weave" and is pronounced *skhet,* like the term for the Egyptian hut that we compared to a Jewish sukkah. Symbolically the Egyptian word reads "the bending sieve of mass" and defines the spiral glyph, ℭ.[22] It is this concept of differentiation relating to matter in its wavelike and particle-like states that we assign to the Sakta god Siva. Since, in the Dogon conception, the po pilu defines the second world of matter, where the perfect order of matter in its wavelike form is first disrupted, then reordered, we interpret that to be the underlying premise behind the myth of the dismemberment of Sati and her reconstitution by Siva. This metaphor, which can be seen to be overtly cosmological in its nature, apparently survived in Egypt as the myth of Osiris and Isis, only with the sexual assignments reversed and with its meanings somewhat distanced from their apparent cosmological origins.

The Dogon phoneme *sa* refers to the process of passing an object from hand to hand and to the difficulties that can arise when trying to do so. Calame-Griaule gives as examples the difficulty of passing a large rock to another person or of passing a heavy bag down from the top of a tree. We can see, based on just the few examples of obstacles we have cited and the subtle nuances of meaning they reflect, why Ganesha's role within the cosmology relates symbolically to the concept of "grayness" and could be a rather complex one to comprehensively summarize.

A more direct association between Sati, Ganesha, and the traditions of the Dogon is preserved in the details of surviving myths that relate to Ganesha. For example, in one telling of the myth, Sati, who has no children of her own, creates Ganesha as a kind of toy doll made from clay, then breathes life into him so that he becomes her real son. One significant detail to be drawn from the myth is that Ganesha calls Sati "Amma," a word that we are told means "mother."[23]

Granoff defines a term from the *Mudgala Purāna* that relates to this Dogon stick figure image of the egg of the world. It is given as *tat tvam asi,* and it has both nonesoteric and esoteric interpretations. In the nonesoteric view, the term is understood to mean "that thou art," a meaning that falls within the same ballpark as the Judaic phrase, "I am that I am." The phrase is derived from an anagram of the Hebrew letters *yud, hay, vav,* and *hay* (pronounced by some as "Yahweh") that can be interpreted to refer to three temporal states of existence: "was, is, will be." From an esoteric perspective, the word *tvat* refers to the elephant head of Ganesha (representing both the female principle and the nonmaterial universe), while *tvam* refers to his body (symbolizing the male principle and our material universe). The word *asi* implies a fundamental equivalence between the two. So once again, the term repeats the essential maxim of our cosmological tradition, "as above, so below." Granoff says that the doctrine asserts that reality lies in a synthesis of two diverging elements that are comparable to spirit and matter and that Ganesha is the one who brings the two together. Hence, the emphasis on an embrace.

16

Elephantine, the Nile Inundation, and the God Hapy

If based on nothing more than name alone, one very likely place in Egypt to look for possible influences of Ganesha and the Sakta goddesses would be Elephantine. Elephantine is an island, known in ancient times as Abu or Yebu, that stands at the northern access to the First Cataract of the Nile River. It was located at what was then the southern border between ancient Egypt and Nubia. It is also located near the Tropic of Cancer, the imaginary line that marks the point at which the sun appears overhead at noon on the summer solstice, before reversing its apparent motion after the longest day of the year. It is the site at which we find the best surviving example of a nilometer, a structure designed to measure and incrementally track the rising level of the Nile river, which was associated with the annual flood or inundation. We know based on previous discussion and references from Budge that the Egyptian word *abu* meant "elephant." However, the root of the word *ab* also meant "tusk," while the root *yeb* could refer both to an elephant and to ivory, a product which is thought to have been traded at Elephantine. One traditional outlook is that Elephantine was so named because the island itself was shaped like an elephant's tusk, an object that is traditionally seen as an archaic symbol of Ganesha.

R. A. Schwaller de Lubicz wrote in his book *Sacred Science: The King of Pharaonic Theocracy* that boats on the Nile displayed symbols that represented Pharaonic nomes or provinces. He says that the image of the elephant was a designation for Elephantine and for the associated first nome of Upper Egypt. In his book he reproduces an image transcribed from ancient Egyptian pottery of one of these boats that carried the elephant symbol. Schwaller de Lubicz writes, "The elephant's presence on these boats . . . brings to mind the epoch when the elephant lived in that country. Indeed, either the symbol was imported by people coming from the south, an assumption which makes little sense, or else the original naming of Elephantine after this animal goes back to a remote epoch when Aswan was not yet the desert of today."[1]

Schwaller de Lubicz's outlook is supported by recent predynastic rock art that has been discovered near Aswan that clearly depicts the image of an elephant and by the statue of a granite elephant that was unearthed on the island of Elephantine in March 2012.

Stephen Quirke tells us that Elephantine was one of the few locales in Egypt that could legitimately claim a heritage that dated back to predynastic times, which he defines in this case to mean 4000 BCE or before. This predynastic tradition centered on a goddess named Satis, who personified the bountiful agricultural produce that resulted from the annual inundation of the Nile. She was seen as having been a war goddess, but her identification with agriculture and fertility could reasonably reflect an identity with Sati and the sister goddesses of our Sakti tradition. Like those goddesses, Satis was paired with another goddess, a goddess of the cataracts (or rapids) named Anuket, whose name actually means "she who embraces." This meaning is sometimes interpreted as having been symbolic of the steep, encircling banks of the Nile River at the First Cataract near Elephantine, rather than as a signature attribute of the goddess. The oldest nilometer at Elephantine is associated with the temple of Satis.

Quirk also mentions in regard to this same goddess, Satis, and the island of Elephantine that there may well be a "precise prehistoric link" to a local goddess named Satet.[2] This outlook is upheld by an online article posted by the Deutsches Archäologisches Institut (German Archaeological Institute), titled "Elephantine." The article states, "The earliest evidence from Elephantine, in the form of pottery finds, points to human presence and activity in the later 5th millennium BC. From about 3300 BC onwards, continuous settlement activity is attested at the island's southern tip, an area that was safe from the inundation. Among the most important features found at Elephantine is the sequence of sanctuaries dedicated to the goddess *Satet* whose cult was related to the flood. It can be traced from the 4th millennium till the forced end of the pagan cults in the early 5th century AD."[3]

We can tentatively correlate this goddess Satet/Satis to our Sakta goddesses based both on the outward similarity of their names and through her association with various signature icons of the Orissa goddesses. One of those would be the potbelly, the clay pot filled with water that represented the goddess and the concept of a womb. In *A Dictionary of Egyptian Gods and Goddesses,* George Hart notes that the name of a goddess he refers to as "the Mistress of Elephantine," originally called Satjit and later Satet, was found on jars from the subterranean galleries of the Step Pyramid at Saqqara (note the *sak* or *saq* phoneme that defines the name of the locale Saqqara). Hart writes, "She is described in the Pyramid Texts as cleansing the King by way of four jars from Elephantine."[4]

Anuket was also known to have been worshipped in Egypt at least since the days of the Old Kingdom, and some researchers surmise that she could have originally been a Nubian goddess. During the Old Kingdom she was seen as a daughter of Re, or Ra, the god of the sun, who we know, when looked at from a cosmic perspective, serves as a symbol for our material universe. By the Middle Kingdom, Anuket and Satis had become associated with the ram god Khnum in a triad of deities. During a later period of Egyptian culture, like the two sister goddesses of the Sakti cult, Satis and Anuket came to be considered symbolic counterparts of Isis and Nephthys, and so can also be associated with the Sirius stars—the symbols of the nonmaterial universe from a cosmic perspective.

In chapter 11 we discussed Dogon and Egyptian concepts of the heliacal rising of Sirius, which was a harbinger of the coming inundation, and how the event was described as representing the meeting of the nonmaterial and material universes. It makes sense that we would find this same symbolic theme reflected at Elephantine, a site that was intimately associated with those same concepts. Perhaps the most obvious expression we can see of this may be through the glyphs of the Egyptian name of the locale itself. Figure 16.1 shows one of the names for Elephantine given by Budge.

Figure 16.1. Egyptian name for Elephantine
(see Budge, *Egyptian Hieroglyphic Dictionary*, 1009)

The name is formed from two twisted rope glyphs (again reminiscent of the Dogon drawing of Amma's universes) joined by the Egyptian ankh glyph (see the middle glyph in figure 16.1), which is traditionally understood to be symbolic of the concept of life. Its use here can be seen to imply a vital joining of two universes. Supportive of this interpretation, the symbolic significance of the city of Elephantine is described in an ancient Egyptian text: "There is a city in the midst of the waters [from which] the Nile rises, named Elephantine. It is the Beginning of the Beginning, the Beginning Nome. . . . It is the joining of the land, the primeval hillock of earth [and] the throne of Re."[5] Here the significance of Elephantine is explained metaphorically in terms of the concept of "earth" (which we see as symbolic both of the material universe and of the earth goddess Tana Penu) and a throne (symbolic in our view of Isis/Sirius, Snodgrass's gateway to the nonmaterial universe, and again of our Sakta goddesses).

Another overt symbolic link between the concept of the Nile inundation and the notion of the meeting of two universes is found in the Egyptian word *heh,* or *hehi,* meaning "the Nile flood" or "inundation." This word is written with the same two twisted rope glyphs and the Egyptian river glyph.[6]

There was another deity, worshipped primarily at Elephantine and at Gebel el Silsila, named Hapi or Hapy, who shares several of Ganesha's attributes, although to our knowledge he was never historically pictured in the form of an elephant. He was the god of the annual flooding of the Nile, and word entries in Budge's dictionary uphold this interpretation. Budge defines the word *hap* to refer to the "Nile river," the words *hap* or *hapi* as a "Nile god," and *hapr* as meaning "inundation."[7]

Hapy was traditionally depicted in ancient Egyptian art with a large belly, long hair, and with pendulous breasts that could have been symbolic of fertility. Quirke tells us that Hapy was of a peculiar character, in that his worship was not conducted through a regular cult with temples and priests, but rather through annual offerings that were made to help promote a good flood.[8] This fact by itself suggests that the tradition associated with Hapy may not have evolved through the same regional cultural or religious processes as did traditions associated with other Egyptian gods or goddesses.

Schwaller de Lubicz, in discussing concepts of pharaonic prehistory and the Ancient Empire in Egypt, refers to Hap the Bull, who "precipitated celestial fire into terrestrial form."[9] This description is a good fit for the cosmological role of Ganesha in his eight incarnations as they relate to the Dogon egg of the world. The reference becomes clearer when we realize that some ancient commentators, such as Strabo, believed that Taurus was originally conceived in India and Egypt to represent an elephant, not a bull. In much the same way that the symbolic commonality between a shrew mouse and an elephant can be seen to rest on the coil of the mouse's tail and the elephant's trunk (each perhaps symbolic of the spiral of Barnard's Loop), so too the common symbolic link between the bull and the elephant rests on their comparable pairs of horns and tusks. In each case, the suggestion is that a change in symbolism may have occurred sometime after the archaic period of our tradition.

The names Hap and Hapy come from the same phonetic root as the Egyptian word *hapt,* discussed in chapter 12, which means "to embrace."[10] Hapy was associated with whirlpools and Osiris and was said to have come through the underworld to Egypt. Stephen Quirke writes in his book *Ancient Egyptian Religion,* "Hapy appears in two and three-dimensional art as a man with pendulous breasts and bearing the plentiful produce of the earth after the inundation [of the Nile]."[11]

We recall that, since earliest times in India, Ganesha was associated with a mouse or a shrew mouse and that Budge defines an archaic Egyptian shrew mouse god named Hetes, based on the same *het* root that he defines to mean "sanctuary" or "temple." Egyptologist Gunter Dreyer of the German Archaeological Institute, in regard to an ancient Egyptian woman of the royal class named Djefatnebti who lived during the Third Dynasty, writes, "Djefatnebti's name appears in black ink inscriptions on a clay beer jar from Elephantine, where she only bears the title *weret hetes* ('great one of the Hetes sceptre'), which was a common title for queens."[12]

This reference becomes more meaningful when we understand that the sceptre was an iconic object that was also traditionally associated with Ganesha, particularly in China and Japan. In Egypt, Budge defines a word for "sceptre" that he pronounces *aab.*[13] It is based on the same phonetic root as an Egyptian word for "elephant"; Budge pronounces it *abu* and spells it using a sceptre glyph, and it is a word that (from our perspective) defines a trailing glyph that is the image of an elephant.[14] A homonym for this same word, *abu,* means "to dance," a symbolic act that is traditionally associated with Ganesha. Similar symbolism is reflected in the language of the Tibetan Na-Khi, where the word for "elephant" also means "to dance."

We have said that the Egyptian words *hap, hapi,* and *hapr* referred to the Nile River, a Nile god, and the concept of the annual inundation of the Nile, respectively. Perhaps a more compelling cosmological link between the Egyptian god Hapy and Ganesha is found with yet another Egyptian word, *skhet,* which Budge also defines to mean "the name of the Nile god" and "inundation." Phonetically, this is the same word that I first associated in *Sacred Symbols of the Dogon* with the Dogon egg of the world or the Calabi-Yau space of string theory,[15] a word whose symbols define it as "the bending sieve of mass" and that qualifies as a defining word for the spiral glyph, ℰ. Since we have already made arguments to demonstrate a relationship between the eight incarnations of Ganesha and the eight stages of this same egg, there is an obvious transitive property at work here. Both Hapy and Ganesha seem to be defined symbolically in relation to the same cosmological structure, the Dogon egg of the world. The mere fact of this commonly shared symbolism argues that Hapy and Ganesha must have also constituted conceptual counterparts to one another.

17

Tamil Word Forms

Dravidian culture and religion, expressed in the Tamil language, are considered to have been major formative influences of the creation traditions and philosophies of India. Both the culture and its religion are understood to have been pre-Vedic, and evidence suggests that their influences were profoundly felt in all regions of India and throughout its history. Appropriate to our studies, the modern centers of ethnic and religious influence of the culture lie in southern and eastern India, in regions that include Orissa, which is also considered to be the home of the Sakti cult. The roots of the Dravidian people were associated with mountains and the rise of agriculture, and Siva is deemed to have originally been a Tamilian/Dravidian deity. Likewise, the tradition gave rise to the goddess Uma, whom we associate with the Dogon deity Amma.

Our success in relating the Tamil word for "elephant," *pilu*, to the Dogon concept of the po pilu suggests that, like the modern-day Turkish language, the Dravidian-based Tamil language might provide yet another source of comparative word meanings that could be useful to our study. Based on that, it seems worthwhile to explore the possible extent of correspondences between Tamil words and key terms of our cosmology. For the purposes of this discussion, Tamil word meanings will be drawn from an online translation site found at www.tamildictionary.com.

Our Tamil word comparisons begin with Amma, the name of

the creator god of the Dogon tradition. The Dogon priests describe Amma as being both male and female, while Brighenti tells us that in the Sakti tradition, Amma is female and identified with an archaic goddess named Uma. There, also, in the Sakti tradition, the processes of creation are understood to derive from a female principle that manifests the male principle, and so Amma, who initiates the processes of creation, would also be female. From this perspective, it makes sense that the Tamil name Amma means "mother." The Dogon priests assign a second set of definitions to the name Amma that mean "to grasp, hold firm, or establish." The similar Hebrew term *amen,* a word that is directly equated to Amma in languages of North Africa, comes from a root that means "to establish" and is used in the context of prayers to mean "so be it" or "make it so." So it seems sensible that in the Tamil language the word *amen* also means "be it so."

The Tamil word *aku,* which means "to become" or "to see," calls to mind the Egyptian and Dogon words for "light," *aakhu* and *ogo.* We previously discussed the Turkish term *ak,* meaning "white," and its possible associations with the light and with the concept of deity in Buddhism and in the Sakti tradition. We also noted how the phoneme *ak* appears in Turkish words for "vulture" and their name for the Dog Star, Sirius, itself.

In the Dogon tradition the term *po pilu* refers to the egg of the world, a fundamental component of the atom-like po. In the Tamil language, the term *pilu* is actually a word for "atom." It is also a term for an "arrow," an object that represented both Tana Penu in India and the mother goddess Net/Neith in predynastic and dynastic Egypt. We have mentioned that the Tamil term *pil,* or *pilu,* can also mean "elephant." The Tamil word *pil* also means "to burst (as a fruit), to break open or to fall off," definitions that seem appropriate to the final "bursting" stage of the Dogon po pilu. The Tamil term *piluvatam* refers to "a system that assumes that the world was made from atoms." We argued in *The Science of the Dogon,* based on biologically related descriptions given by the Dogon priests, that the Dogon term *kikinu* referred to the genes of a cell that first divide during the process of meiosis, then combine to form a zygote. The Dogon word *ki* means "nose" and is pictured as a pointed nose-like shape that looks like a single gene as it divides during the processes of biological reproduction.[1] It could be this process that is referred to by the Tamil word *kinu,* which means "to cut into slices."

The Tamil term *penu,* which we associate with the archaic sister goddesses Dharni Penu and Tana Penu, means "to honor and respect, honor as a father and a mother, take care of, nurture, and cherish." These are all meanings that fit well with the concepts of mothers, revered ancestors, mother goddesses, and the notion of the embrace that we associate with the hugging Ganeshas, and with the dual arms on the pillars at Gobekli Tepe. It comes from the root word *pen,* which means "woman" or "girl."

In Egypt and among the Dogon we equate the root *tem* with the idea of "completion" and with the scientific concept of mass and the cosmological concept of earth. The term *earth* is given both in a cosmological sense and in relation to the actual terra firma of our world. *Tem* is also the Egyptian phonetic value that seems to relate to so many of the symbolic elements that are found at Gobekli Tepe. Tem is also understood in Egypt as the name of an archaic earth god, essentially a male counterpart to Tana Penu in the Sakti tradition. In the Tamil language, the word *tem* means "place, location, room, land or country."

We have said that the Sakta goddess Tana Penu may relate to the mythical teachers of the Dogon, who were said to have brought skills of civilization such as weaving and agriculture to humanity and to have eventually left. From that perspective, Tamil words that are based on the phonetic root *ta* seem to make sense. These include the root *ta* itself, which means "to give, grant or bestow," the word *tanai,* which refers to the concept of "cloth," and the word *tana,* which means "to depart" or "leave."

We have made reference here and in *The Cosmological Origins of*

Myth and Symbol to a priestly tribe from the Tibetan/Chinese border called the Na-Khi, or Naxi, whose name implies celebration of the principle of the mother goddess Na. This is the same essential principle that we see reflected in the concept of the fertility cult of the female yoginis within the Sakti cult of Orissa. In the Tamil language, we encounter the term *nacci,* reminiscent of the name Naxi, which refers to "a class of seven female deities." The name is founded on the same root as the Tamil term *nacai,* which defines the concepts of "desire, lust, and affection." We also commented that the Na-Khi define their honored ancestor-teachers as Mu ancestors, a term that, if we entertain the notion that ours might not have been the first civilization to have ever emerged on our planet, could harken back to the memory of an earlier society. Perhaps in that same regard, the Tamil word *mu* refers to "that which was before."

In *The Science of the Dogon,* we mentioned that the native Maori of New Zealand define a concept called po that is quite similar to the Dogon atom-like component of matter, also called po. However, for the Maori, the term also has connotations that relate to the concept of death. (Dogon and Egyptian references are to "primordial time," a period that fell conceptually "before creation" and "before life.") Based on multiple discrete definitions, we correlated the Dogon word *po* to the Egyptian terms *pau, paut,* and *pauti.* From this perspective, it seems understandable that the Tamil term *pautti* also means "death." A related Tamil word, *pautikam,* is a name for the Rig Veda, one of the eight Puranas and one of the earliest known ancient texts.

The Tamil language includes a word, *nunukkam,* outwardly formed from two or more cosmological roots that are familiar to our studies of cosmology. This word defines the concepts of "fineness" or "minuteness," comparable to how we might describe the processes of creation in the microcosm. A related term, *nunakkam,* refers to "a flexure or movement" that calls to mind the complex pivoting motion that characterizes the earliest stages of creation in our cosmologies.

There are other Tamil words whose meanings fit the expected

mold of our cosmology without the need for special interpretation and so reflect the likely influence of this same system of cosmology. One is the word *stupi,* which refers to "the top of a temple," comparable to the idea of a Buddhist stupa or a Christian steeple. Another is the word Om, which is defined as a mystic name for a deity and can be applied to Vishnu, to Siva, or to Brahma. These meanings could also relate to the word *olam,* which means "sound, noise or invocation" and defines the very essence of the Buddhist concept of Om. And finally there is a Tamil word, *meru,* which refers to the familiar mythical Mount Meru, a symbol of cosmology that was said to reside at the center of the Earth.

18

A Rationale
for the Civilizing Plan

At this point in our explorations, there is hardly a concept, term, symbol, deity, or mythic theme of the classic ancient cosmologies whose meanings we cannot demonstrate broad agreement about among the various traditions we have studied. Clearly what we have been exploring are not simply elements of independent traditions that were somehow incidentally similar, but rather a coherent set of related symbols that were commonly shared by the cultures. The coherence of these symbols, the concepts they represent, and the ways in which they convey their meanings strongly suggests that they were part of a single, well-defined system that was meant to convey and perpetuate specific meanings.

It is the consensus view of these cultures that key civilizing skills were intentionally taught to them in ancient times and that one primary effect of those teachings was to lift their cultures upward from a pastoral state of hunting and gathering to the status of farmers and city dwellers. Along with this change in cultural status came the first evidence of cultivated grains, domesticated animals, ritual and civic centers, metallurgy, and stone masonry. To one degree or another, each culture we have studied expressly assigns credit for these developments to sometimes-deified ancestor-teachers who are flatly said to have brought these civilizing skills to humanity.

Perhaps our best indicator of who that outside presence may have been comes out of comparisons between what the Dogon and the Buddhists both assert to be true about their traditions. In order to put these views in perspective, we first need to review some pertinent facts about these traditions. To begin with, we know with certainty that the cosmology that Marcel Griaule documented for the Dogon is a legitimate one because it presents such a very close match for the Buddhist stupa cosmology, which is long known, well defined, and academically accepted. We know based on discussion in *The Cosmological Origins of Myth and Symbol* that the Dogon cosmology must also be an ancient tradition because, in relation to Buddhism, its pertinent elements were firmly documented by around 400 BCE. It would be difficult to argue that either the Dogon or the Buddhists could have adopted their tradition wholesale from the other because the two systems are defined in markedly different languages. In fact, the many cosmological words that are shared commonly by the Dogon and the ancient Egyptians argue that the Dogon version of the tradition must actually date from an era prior to 400 BCE, since the Egyptian hieroglyphic language fell largely out of use by around 700 BCE. Our ability to match these two traditions in the modern era implies that both cultures—the Buddhists and the Dogon—were able to preserve the many intimate details of their tradition and pass them down intact from generation to generation for a period of at least 2,500 years. This fact alone lends strong testimony to the very great coherence of the symbolic system itself.

When we finally do arrive at the conceptual bottom of these traditions, we find that the Dogon and the Buddhists each credit the same unlikely source: they say that this civilizing plan, which they each characterize as an instructed system, was revealed to humanity by knowledgeable teachers who were not themselves human. Adrian Snodgrass flatly asserts this viewpoint in the very first pages of his book *The Symbolism of the Stupa*. He writes, "The adequate, or sacred symbol, is deemed to have been 'given'; it is revealed to the tradition from a non-human source. It is adequate precisely because it is not a mere contrivance of the human mind."[1]

The Dogon priests also expressly credit this system of knowledge to nonhumans, but go one step further to describe their ancestral teachers as spiritual (nonmaterial) beings who were very concerned about the possible harmful effects that long-term interaction with them could have on creatures of flesh and blood, such as ourselves. Like many other ancient cultures, the Dogon perceived these nonhuman teachers as being godlike. However, the Dogon had the presence of mind to actually question their teachers on this point, and they were told no, their teachers were not gods, but if the Dogon preferred, they could think of them as "agents of god."

The fact that the Dogon and Buddhists are in agreement about this very controversial aspect of their tradition leaves us with only two working alternatives: We can adopt the outlook that each culture managed to keep the many subtle details of their teachings straight for generation after generation, but then somehow misremembered this one critical point, both choosing to misrepresent the perceived nonhuman nature of their teachers as if it were factual, rather than as mythical or metaphoric. Or, as we have done with any number of other cross-confirming, scientifically sensible aspects that the two traditions share, we can simply take these statements at face value and accept them as being factual and mutually corroborating.

For some time, the suggestion that the Dogon ancestor-teachers could have been nonmaterial beings presented a thorny conundrum for our studies, beyond the obviously controversial nature of the outlook itself. After all, it might seem reasonable that well-intentioned visitors who were "aliens" in the traditional sci-fi sense could have travelled here from the relatively nearby star system of Sirius. Taken in that context, the important role that Sirius played in the cosmologies of various ancient cultures would make sense. But the Dogon and Buddhist notion of nonmaterial beings suggests interdimensionality, not other-worldliness, and so of itself would have no requisite link to another star system. Looked at in this way, the question, "Why Sirius?" stood as a kind of conceptual roadblock to acceptance of the Dogon outlook. However, when we moved to a discussion of paired structures in the galactic realm whose details are also cross-corroborated among multiple traditions, Snodgrass's claims for the existence of a sun door between our material universe and its non-material twin, seemingly located at Sirius, brought the idea of Sirius back into significance in relation to teachers who were ostensibly interdimensional in nature.

Another approach would be to dismiss out of hand any suggestion of nonhuman involvement in our history. But given the consistently scientific nature of various cosmological references in the traditions we are studying, almost any competing answer we could reasonably propose for their origin (ones with the potential to explain the apparent scientific correctness of those references) would necessarily fall outside the boundaries of any traditionally acceptable paradigm. The hard truth is that we simply have no credible candidates in archaic times who could have conceived of and/or globally communicated this type of scientifically correct civilizing plan. We could argue that the plan originated with a pre–ice age civilization, but the quality of information that is reflected within the civilizing plan, especially that which relates to the structure of parallel universes, implies a space-capable culture that, in terms of credibility, would be as problematic for a traditional researcher as sci-fi aliens.

However, in support of this controversial Dogon/Buddhist view-point, we again have an ability to infer what is likely to be correct. The cosmology starts with ancient descriptions of matter that seem to correctly define the concepts of an atom and its constituent elements. Working conceptually downward from there, we encounter descriptions that are an arguable match for the best modern scientific theories on the structure of matter, quantum theory, and string theory. The cosmology defines matter in terms of waves and particles and defines particles in relation to the vibration of strings, and it rests on a fundamental principle of duality. Within the cosmology, these definitions are presented hand in hand with an arguably correct description of the beginnings of our universe, attributed to an event comparable to the big bang and predicated on the notion of an expanding universe. So from several different perspectives our ancient cosmology looks like reasonable science.

It is safe to say that no modern scientist who studies the processes of creation could miss the obvious outward similarity of orbiting electrons to orbiting planets. So the signature theme of the ancient cosmologies, "as above, so below," should not present any real problem to a scientifically minded researcher. Nor could any astrophysicist be truly surprised by the notion that multiple universes or twin universes might potentially exist or, given current theories of dark matter and dark energy, that a universe could exist that would be of a nonmaterial nature. The point is that the essential concepts that underlie these ancient creation traditions all seem fairly reasonable from a modern scientific perspective.

The prospect of direct parallelism between the processes of the macrocosm and the microcosm is also a scientifically tenable one. We are told that the notion of multiple universes is almost requisite to modern theories of the formation of our universe. However, in many cases, the information that is put forth in the ancient references we cite seems to have been given from a perspective of assured knowledge, not tentative theory. For example, the Dogon flatly state that there are 266 fundamental particles of matter. They define a forthright process by which waves of matter are said to be transformed into particles. They describe the changes in state that a wave passes through on its way to forming the Calabi-Yau space. Furthermore, their conception of how universes evolve is given in a way that, if correct, effectively unifies the processes of the macrocosm, the microcosm, and the biology of life in relation to a common heliacal structure comparable to DNA. What we are dealing with here must either be the product of an unbelievably prescient ancient imagination or else it must reflect underlying truths that were actually known to someone in ancient times.

Furthermore, there are certain aspects of creation that are defined by our ancient tradition, but that go beyond topics that are typically addressed by modern astrophysicists. These include concepts of how a simple act of perception can transform matter's wavelike behavior into that of particles. They include the question of what conditions may have preceded or catalyzed the big bang. They encompass a discussion of what lies outside our known universe. Not only are such issues actually addressed in our ancient tradition, but the answers it provides, as noted here, also have the same ring of scientific reasonableness as the many other, more immediately verifiable aspects of the tradition, those that do fall within the scope of our own immediate understanding. The clear suggestion is that whoever was behind this tradition knew what they were talking about. Since we have no known candidates in archaic times who, based on the traditional paradigm, could have reasonably been in possession of this knowledge, all we are left with are those who are unknown to us. From that perspective, a group of well-intentioned interdimensional teachers seems as likely (or as unlikely) a candidate as any other.

The idea of intention may also be a key to a broader understanding here, because, as we have commented before in previous volumes of this series, what we see consistently reflected in the Dogon traditions in relation to their ancestor-teachers are only the very best of intentions. As Griaule describes them, interactions between the Dogon and their ancestor-teachers seem to have always been conducted on a basis of concerned truthfulness. In every case, the definitions we see reflected in the Dogon and Egyptian symbols and drawings seem to have been carefully considered, thoughtfully conceived, well presented, and uniformly accurate.

We have so far become aware of two alternate points of entry into this tradition. The first is an exceedingly archaic one; it long predates written language and takes its outward representations in aniconic forms such as standing stones and stone cairns. This is the tradition that we associate with Gobekli Tepe. It likely corresponds to the honored First Time of the Egyptians and to the first transmissions of knowledge to mankind by Buddha. We see evidence of it reflected in the modern Turkish language and in the Dravidian-based Tamil language. We see cosmologically significant phonetic roots from these languages reflected in a wide range of symbolic terms of the Dogon and in correlated Egyptian hieroglyphic words.

We have demonstrated that many of the structural elements at Gobekli Tepe reflect the characteristic symbolism of the Sakta mother goddesses, beginning with the placement of stone pillars in a circle. When we compare the Gobekli Tepe structures to the archaic form of the chaitya sanctuaries, the suggestion arises that a wooden stupa, long-since deteriorated, might once have been housed within each circle of pillars. The carved images on the stone pillars at Gobekli Tepe present a mix of symbolic forms whose meanings survive in later traditions. We see the *H* and the sun glyph shapes as being symbolic of the two paired universes, one of a nonmaterial nature and the other material. Based on recurrent word meanings found in several different languages, the carved disembodied arms, which are tentatively interpreted by the excavators of Gobekli Tepe as referring to "ancestors," seem to correspond to the notion of an embrace between those two universes, which is implied in other aspects of our tradition. Cross-cultural ancient references lead us to understand the three carved hemispheres or dome shapes to be representative of the concept of a temple or sanctuary, the place at which, in many of our traditions, the two universes (characterized as "divine" and "mundane" or "heavenly" and "earthly") are understood to come together. In accordance with archaic symbolic practices of the Sakti cult and later symbolism known from other traditions we are studying (such as the Chinese zodiac), we interpret the animal images at Gobekli Tepe as being symbolic of stages and/or concepts of creation. Ancient Egyptian homonyms for animal names suggest that these may have constituted a kind of protowriting, in which the name of the animal also stood for a term of cosmology. These were perhaps used to identify specific concepts that may have been taught at that location.

Beyond the actual locale of Gobekli Tepe, the rare extant artifacts that might be attributed to this archaic tradition, such as the enigmatic Sphinx in Egypt or the ancient structures at Çatalhüyük or Machu Picchu, argue that this tradition emerged sometime shortly after the end of the last ice age, some eleven thousand years ago. That timing supports the controversial outlook that a well-intentioned outside presence (earthly or otherwise) may have made a deliberate attempt to assist cultures in the Gobekli Tepe region in their recovery from a global catastrophe that coincided with the end of the last ice age. We know that Gobekli Tepe is located in the same vicinity where we find the first evidence of cultivated grains, domesticated animals, and metallurgy. This again supports the idea that civilizing skills may have been intentionally introduced (or as Dogon definitions imply, reintroduced) there. Francesco Brighenti tells us that DNA and linguistic studies show that these same civilizing skills spread outward in all directions from this definable point of origin, in tandem with words and rituals similar to those that characterize the Sakti tradition.

Because of their inferred stellar alignments, the suggestion is that at least the ground plan for the pyramids of Giza also dates from this archaic era. It seems consistent, both with the known practices of the Sakti and Dogon traditions and with overt evidence relating to the carving of the Sphinx, that natural outcroppings, caves, and standing stones may have been originally adapted to mark ritual sites, sites that may also have had stellar correlations, and that these sites came to define the future locations of later structures, such as the Giza pyramids. Meanwhile, within that mindset it seems reasonable to associate the noticeably higher quality of craftsmanship of the Great Pyramid with the teachers (as compared with later, arguably less grandly conceived and less well-constructed pyramids), whose obvious skill level we see reflected in other aspects of the cosmology and civilizing plan.

Surviving evidence currently allows us to trace the early archaic incarnation of the tradition forward no more than about fifteen hundred years beyond its initial inception, after which, due largely to lack of surviving evidence, we simply lose our ability to track it. We argued previously that the nature of the esoteric tradition itself implies that there could have been competition between two ancient groups—one devoted to helping humanity and one not—and there could have been a desire on the part of the ancient ancestor-teachers to hide their instructional efforts from that second group. As we have suggested, this same desire could possibly explain the later deliberate, careful burial of the Gobekli Tepe site. However, other aspects of the tradition, such as the megalithic design of the pyramids, were clearly aimed at longevity and an implied desire that the tradition be communicated forward to later eras such as our own. From that perspective, the burial of the site might be interpreted as part of an original design, a choice implemented after the practical instructional purposes of the structures had already been fulfilled, as a way of preserving the site for posterity. If that were the case, then we might well expect to eventually uncover similar carefully buried centralized mountaintop sanctuaries in other regions of the world.

A second, later point of entry to our tradition, concurrent with the dawn of the historical era, was opened to us through the onset of writing around 3000 BCE. The tradition of this era is carried forward to us through written texts, the ruins of megalithic stone structures, stone engravings, carvings, and artwork that has survived the various ravages of time. This is the era of ancient Egypt, the Vedic, Hindu, and Buddhist traditions, ancient China, and the other related traditions we are studying.

Although there seem to have been significant differences in the way these two widely distanced eras of our tradition (archaic and historic) were implemented, certain shared attributes argue that the two were inextricably linked. The first of these lies with the unarguable emphasis that is evident in both eras on the geometric figures of the circle, square, and hemisphere. We find the shapes of hemispheres prominently carved in proximity with squares on the Gobekli Tepe pillars, and we find imagery of circles and squares employed exhaustively in the cosmological traditions of virtually every culture we are studying, defined in symbolic relation to one another.

In both eras there was also specific animal-related symbolism assigned to serpents, to vultures and other similar birds of prey, to bulls and cows, to geese and other water birds, and to scorpions. This symbolism serves to overtly associate the archaic period with both India (where animals came to be symbolic determinatives of deities) and with the later predynastic and earliest dynastic periods in Egypt (where deities came to be depicted in art with animal heads). We know that many of these same animals were adopted as icons of the earliest rulers in virtually every ancient tradition we are studying, which served to affiliate those rulers with the gods of their cultures.

There was also a tradition of megalithic stone construction and refined stone carving that made its first appearance at Gobekli Tepe and that can be seen as a unifying feature of cultures worldwide in both eras. Stoneworking techniques and architectural forms that are sometimes shared by widely distant cultures have long been a source of perplexity to researchers of ancient cultures, but might make better sense when viewed in the context of a common instructional tradition.

The practice of ancestor worship that is exhibited among many preliterate cultures is also one that serves to bind the archaic and historic eras of our tradition together. In Egypt, India, and China, and among cultures like the Dogon and the Na-Khi, there is a pervasive cultural sense of looking nostalgically backward to an idealized golden age. This outlook is reflected in a strong cultural desire to honor a revered set of founding ancestors and also to actively

justify significant new acts in relation to some ancient, almost paren-
tal authority that somehow still holds ultimate sway. In Egypt, such
authority is overtly assigned to the remote period of the First Time,
an era whose existence is supported quasi-historically through surviving king lists. In addition to the sequential names of rulers, these lists
give an ostensible length of reign in years for each king, and when we
accumulate a total for those reigns, the summed span of years again
points to beginnings in the approximate era of Gobekli Tepe.

As I have suggested, in Egypt there are proposed astronomical
alignments associated with the pyramids and the Sphinx at Giza that
mark a precessional era in which the sun on the summer equinox rose
between the Earth and the constellation of Leo. Based on computer
models that can regress the stars backward in time to that configuration, the timing also points suggestively to the very same era in which
Gobekli Tepe is estimated to have been built. From that perspective,
Giza serves as a kind of geodetic clock, set to a moment in time that
marks the earlier era of our tradition.

We can well imagine that any effort to provide aid to a struggling
humanity might have focused first on education. Because such efforts
would have predated writing, what we know of any ancient process of
instruction comes to us necessarily through what are essentially folk
stories that survive from culture to culture. Certain themes are common to these stories, and they often include mention of mountaintop
sanctuaries where deities were supposed to have lived and where certain select people were said to have been taken in archaic times by
godlike authorities. The Dogon priests describe a carefully considered
policy on the part of their ancestor-teachers, in which a small number
of tribespeople were to be sequestered in a remote locale for direct
instruction in various civilizing skills and then returned back to the
tribe, charged with the task of passing those same skills along to other
members of their community.

The Buddhist tradition also holds that knowledge was deliberately disseminated to mankind in ancient times at a remote mountain

location referred to as Vulture Peak, a term that aptly describes the sanctuary at Gobekli Tepe. Likewise, it is the Sakti cult of Orissa, a tradition of India that is understood to have been ancestral to the Vedics, Hindus, and Buddhists, that provides us with a coherent set of concepts, practices, beliefs, words, and symbols that link credibly back to what we see at Gobekli Tepe and forward to each of the other traditions we are studying.

There is an apocryphal biblical account in which Enoch, an archaic ancestor of Noah, was ostensibly taken up to heaven and then later returned home, where he reported the numerous wonders he had seen there. There were tales in the Tibetan traditions of ancient mountaintop sanctuaries or temples that were the reported domains of divine teachers. In Peru, there are numerous well-known mountaintop sanctuaries whose uncertain origins appear to stretch back to the earliest days of humanity. Similar reports of other mythical mountain top sanctuaries are found in the myths of many different cultures worldwide.

The structures that are currently under excavation at Gobekli Tepe would seem to meet the criteria for one of these mythical instructional sanctuaries. Support for this interpretation begins with the physical evidence that has been uncovered at the site, much of which points reasonably to that conclusion. First, there are few signs of habitation at the site, and so the possibility that it might have served as a dwelling place is effectively ruled out. Researchers have not found the discarded refuse of feasts or of clay pots for the storage of wine or beer at Gobekli Tepe, so it was not likely used as a ceremonial center. Based on its mountaintop placement it was not well located to have served as a center of commerce or agriculture. The site does not include features that suggest that it could have been used as a fortress. Some researchers have proposed astronomical alignments for the megalithic stone pillars, but the site does not include overt features that we would associate with an astronomical observatory. Whatever theoretical purpose we might propose for the ancient site also requires a sensible rationale to explain why bands of hunter-gatherers would have come together to build it in the first place.

As I have mentioned, at Gobekli Tepe we have circles of megalithic pillars so very ancient that they actually seem to predate evidence of the tools (let alone the practiced skills) required to build them. On the pillars we have the earliest known examples of fine stone carving, including inscribed carvings, figures of animals carved in the round, and more refined carvings done in relief. These reflect a degree of artistry that should only have been acquired over time. It's clear that at least the minimal technology required to transport the immense pillar stones the distance from where they were quarried to where they were erected must have also existed here. Unlike in later Egypt where quarried stone could be transported with relative ease on boats along the Nile River, here the stones must have been moved overland and up and down mountain hillsides. All of this is reflective of a sophisticated stoneworking tradition that apparently grew up here. We would expect such a tradition to have left evidence of its progression in the geological layers of the site, but few tools of the trade have actually been uncovered here.

The very words used to define the Gobekli Tepe site reflect aspects of our cosmological tradition. These begin with the name of the site itself, traditionally translated as "potbelly hill," since the potbelly was an archaic symbol of the mother goddess in our Sakti tradition. And because of the multiplicity of meanings that attach to the Turkish words *gobekli* and *tepe,* there are more than a few alternate translations for the term that serve as conceptual links to our tradition. From one perspective it was a "hill with a navel," the symbolic definition of a Buddhist stupa. From another perspective, the Turkish term *tepe* could mean "topknot," a meaning that is again used to symbolize a stupa. Because the Turkish word *gobek* refers to the "midpoint" and the word *tepe* relates both to the peak of a hill or mountain and to a Turkish term for "dome," the name can also be seen to be related to concepts of ascension in Buddhism, a process that Adrian Snodgrass explicitly defines in terms of rising to the peak of a dome. Phonetic similarity to the Turkish word for "dog," *kopek,* suggests symbolism that could be associated with the stars of Sirius.

Correlations between the Turkish and Egyptian words *tepe* and *tepi* bring us to another set of meanings that could be associated with our cosmology. These include meanings that relate to the notion of "ancestors" and with the concept of a primeval or "first" time. Egyptian *tep* words also include meanings that could be suggestive of ancient sky-burial rituals and of the box or coffin associated with the creation myth of Osiris.

Archaic word forms found in the Egyptian, Dogon, Turkish, Sanskrit, and Tamil languages suggest that over time, a divergence may have occurred in the pronunciation of certain cosmological terms. One aspect of this apparent divergence centers on the archaic Egyptian shrine glyph, whose pronunciation may have been originally comparable to the throaty "ch" sound in Hebrew. Terms like Ganesha suggest that this phoneme survived in India pronounced as a *G,* while related Egyptian words seem to have emerged as an *H.* This divergence left us with a set of words relating to the *ga/ge/get* pronunciation in the languages of some cultures such as India and the Dogon, *ha/he/het* in other cultures like ancient Egypt, and *ch/cha* in yet a third set of languages such as ancient Hebrew and with the name of the archaic temple form *chaitya.* These apparent differences in pronunciation create difficulties in correlating certain archaic terms between cultures.

These differences in pronunciation seem to be exacerbated by apparent changes in the grammatical interpretation of ancient Egyptian words between archaic and more modernized word forms. So without an awareness of these apparent equivalencies, it becomes problematic to try to relate seemingly archaic names like Ga nu sa Ast to a more immediately recognizable modernized pronunciation of Het Penu Sa Ast or from Het Pet Kai to a modernized Het Pet Ka Yah. Yet it would appear that comparable terms such as Ganesa/

Ganesha and Gobekli survived in the languages of India and Turkey.

Evolution of form constitutes a similar problem in aspects of the tradition other than simply in terms of language. Perhaps the most obvious example is the multiplicity of localized forms that deities can take within various cultures. We see this to a minor extent in Egypt, where alternate outlooks on the Ennead and Ogdoad deities were emphasized in their own cult centers, where different creator-gods were emphasized in different eras, and where, in certain contexts, deities like Hathor and Isis could be seen as effective surrogates of one another. But the problem grows to much grander proportions in India, where hundreds or even thousands of different names can sometimes be assigned to conceptually similar deities.

If we were to summarize how the various incarnations of our tradition might relate to one another historically, there is a sensible viewpoint from which Gobekli Tepe represented a centrally located archaic instructional center whose purpose was to establish (or perhaps reestablish) a set of civilizing skills among a populace of hunter-gatherers. If we take the Dogon and Buddhist statements at face value, a group of well-intentioned ancient instructors who were themselves not human brought class-sized groups of initiates from surrounding regions to Gobekli Tepe for the purpose of teaching them a set of skills required for the establishment of agriculture. Instruction of these skills was framed within the context of a scientifically based creation tradition, designed to help humanity comprehend its own place within the larger structures of the universe.

The multiple sets of circular stone pillars under excavation at Gobekli Tepe, which were built over a period of time, seem likely to have served as hands-on practical projects for these initiates, through which to hone the quarrying, stoneworking, construction, and carving skills they had learned. The structures likely also provided classroom space in which to house later groups of initiates who would follow. They also likely served as a working example for the initiates of a ritual sanctuary.

The Gobekli Tepe site exhibits many of the signature attributes of the Sakti cult, whose modern-day center of worship is in the Orissa region of southeastern India. The Sakti tradition is widely deemed to be exceedingly ancient and has its historical roots to the northwest of India, in the general direction of the Fertile Crescent and western Iran, nearest to where the Turkish site of Gobekli Tepe is located. The cult is associated with the same agricultural and civilizing skills that are thought to have originated in vicinities near Gobekli Tepe. The Sakti cult is an acknowledged predecessor of the Vedic, Hindu, and Buddhist traditions, and its early widespread influence is attested throughout India. So the suggestion is that this cult is a likely descendant of that original instructional tradition at Gobekli Tepe.

In later eras, Buddhism is understood to have migrated from India to China and Japan and to have firmly taken root there, during the same era when numerous other religions simply did not succeed in doing so. The academic question arises as to why Buddhism managed to thrive there, while other religions did not. Based on our perspective and the geographic location of Gobekli Tepe, the suggestion is that China (and perhaps Japan) may have been a recipient of this same instructed tradition from Gobekli Tepe. This implies that the later Buddhist tradition may have been able to thrive in China so easily because, having seemingly derived from a common source, it may have been a compatible match for traditions already in existence there. (I discuss many points of commonality between the earliest Chinese cosmology and the Dogon/Egyptian cosmological model in *China's Cosmological Prehistory.*)

We have demonstrated numerous parallels between Sakti cult practices and those found in ancient Egypt. These include commonly shared myths; word forms; deity names, roles, and attributes; and other significant details of cosmology. They center first and foremost on archaic traditions documented at Elephantine and on the Sakta-like Egyptian sister goddesses Satis and Anuket and the Ganesha-like Egyptian god of the Nile, Hapy, who were celebrated there. Lack of surviving evidence makes it uncertain whether these similarities may have stemmed from parallelism in the two traditions, reflective of a commonly shared origin, or whether the influences of the Sakti cult in India might have extended themselves as far as Egypt during predynastic times. In either case, what seems clear is that the myth of Osiris and Isis in Egypt seems further removed in time from its apparent cosmological origins than that of Siva, Sati, and Ganesha in India.

It also seems clear that a significant number of Dogon cosmological words relate to the Dravidian tradition. So, to the extent that the Dogon and Egyptian cultures and cosmologies positively align with one another, we might assume that what we can demonstrate to be true for the Dogon may also have been true for the ancient Egyptians, and so infer possible Dravidian influences there, also. Through Ganesha, whose symbolism is unquestionably central to the cosmological traditions of India, we can demonstrate fundamental commonalities between the innermost traditions of cosmology in India and those of the Dogon. Dogon definitions of the po pilu concept provide us with an entirely credible rationale for interpreting Ganesha's symbolism in India. This perspective is wholly affirmed by the effective match that demonstrably exists between the Buddhist stupa and Dogon granary shrine forms and their related cosmologies.

In other words, there is a coherent perspective from which to suggest that all of the traditions we have been comparing relate to one another ancestrally and that this common ancestry began at Gobekli Tepe. In its earliest form, the tradition was rooted in concepts of a feminine principle that manifests a male principle and took its practical expression in a Neith-like/Sati-like mother goddess whose role it was to create matter and evoke the material universe. The tradition appears to have been aniconic in its earliest presentation, but from the beginning its words and concepts were closely linked to animals. The tradition was characterized by high mountaintop sanctuaries and associated with circles of standing stones.

The three hemispheric glyphs carved on one of the Gobekli Tepe pillars suggest that the dome, representing a space within which the divine and mundane universes meet, held a symbolic place in the earliest conceptualization of a sanctuary or temple. The appearance of three glyph-like hemisphere figures side by side implies that concepts of ascension similar to those described by Adrian Snodgrass may have been original to the tradition. When taken in combination with Budge's three-term archaic sanctuary names (given in relation to three astronomic bodies or three deities), these figures imply that symbolic correspondences to Sirius, Barnard's Loop, and Orion's Belt may have also been part of the initial conception of the tradition. We see an outward match for the three hemispheres reflected in the form of a three-stone cairn, a structure that, through its symbolism, links conceptually forward to the Buddhist stupa. The practice of building three-stone cairns represents just one of many points of commonality between the archaic traditions found at Gobekli Tepe and the modern-day Dogon tribe.

We see the significance of Sirius, Orion, and Barnard's Loop reflected in nearly every ancient creation tradition we are studying, although to my knowledge, the symbolism that relates to Barnard's Loop (or for that matter, even its existence) has generally not been recognized for what the Dogon claim it to be. Nonetheless, we see that the concept of a cosmic wheel, the notion of a chariot, and references to the wheel of a chariot are quite evident among the myths of many ancient cultures. Likewise, the concept of a triad or trinity, as found in Christianity, is central to many of the later religions of the world. It seems likely that the concept is rooted in archaic symbolism that relates to ascension and to domes.

It is apparent that a tangible change in symbolism occurred within the tradition at some point prior to 3000 BCE, and we see several specific indications of this. First, in many cultures, what had originally been an aniconic tradition began to express itself iconically. A symbolic system in which animals had been directly affiliated with cosmological words and concepts was replaced, in India and in Egypt and in other contemporaneous cultures, with one in which animals began to be used primarily as determinatives of now-anthropomorphized deities. Symbolic roles previously played by somewhat generic, quasi-mythical ancestors were now performed by personified and named deities. Through myth, the attributes and actions of these deities came to reflect stages and concepts of cosmology, and the associated animals were largely reduced to the status of avatars. Mythic traditions of even later cultures like ancient Greece took this basic trend yet another step further by focusing on the soap-opera-like frailties of these now-humanized pantheons of gods and goddesses.

Among the changes that occurred between the archaic and historic eras of our creation tradition, certain symbolic associations seem to have been reassigned or transposed. But many of these reassignments took place not just within a single culture, but also often across the broad spectrum of these ancestrally related cultures. First, what had originally been cast as an overtly feminine tradition, characterized by a mother goddess, fertility cults, and yoginis, was by later eras transformed into one that was paternalistic in outlook, initiated by creator-gods instead of goddesses, and in which the original goddesses were now demoted to the role of consorts to those gods. For example, the mother goddess Uma appears to have been reinterpreted as a male god Amma or Amen. In some cultures, like the Dogon, Amma was considered to be of a dual nature, both male and female. Osiris in Egypt took on many of the archaic attributes of Sati, with Isis or Hathor as his consort, while in India the primary focus shifted in large part to Sati's male counterpart, Siva.

Symbolism that, based on the meaning of words like *penu,* must have been originally assigned to animals like the shrew mouse, was transferred to another symbolically similar animal, the elephant. Ganesha was widely understood to have lost his original head and then acquired a new one, the head of a white elephant, and the old symbolism was sufficiently well established to require explanation through mythic narrative. Birds, which in older representations of the cosmology stood as metaphors for the final stages of creation, later came to bear symbolic relationship to the male creator-gods, who, in the more recent presentation, were now credited with having initiated the processes of creation. Because of that transposition, some birds now seemingly came to correspond to the earliest stages of creation.

By dynastic times in Egypt, archaic ritual structures that most often took rounded forms (as seen in the circular pillars of Gobekli Tepe and of archaic chaitya temples and in very early architecture in Egypt) had largely become squared, especially in Egypt. The Dogon granary, which we take to represent an archaic structural form, culminated in a round base, while the Buddhist stupa, which we interpret as a somewhat more recent version of the same form, was brought to completion with a base that was square. In the archaic Dogon system of agriculture, land plots were originally plowed in a circular or spiral shape, while in the later, fully articulated well-field system (a system that was also known in China) they were defined by square plots. Archaic circular architectural features at Saqqara in Egypt were seemingly never replicated, but were apparently supplanted in dynastic times with squared architecture. In fact, even the Great Pyramid itself is traditionally understood to present the geometry of a hemisphere that has again been squared.

Yet another major change in the symbolic structure of the tradition, dating to the same approximate era of 3000 BCE, came with the development of written language. The earliest symbolic languages were set down with glyphs that often appeared to have been adopted wholesale from a preexisting cosmology. More than a few cultures overtly claim to have received their earliest systems of writing from knowledgeable teachers or deities, and so it is arguably in relation to this onset of writing that the active hand of a capable teacher is most overtly seen.

The Dogon priests say that a final turning point in their ancestral creation tradition came when their revered teachers either chose to leave or were forced to leave by some unnamed outside influence. Similar tales are told in the Americas about revered, benevolent bearded gods who eventually chose to depart, making solemn promises to someday return. In so doing, they may have inadvertently set the scene for a regrettable case of mistaken identity, whereby Spanish warriors were later taken for beneficent returning gods. We see support for the Dogon scenario in Old Testament passages relating to the jealous God of the Judeo-Christian tradition, who, at the time of Moses and the Exodus, is said to have unleashed a series of plagues against the Egyptian gods, expressly forbidding the Israelites from "having any other gods before him."

This final shared theme of the traditions we are studying, defined in relation to the regretful departure of a culture's mythical instructors, in some ways neatly closes the circle of comparisons we have been presenting here. We have been able to demonstrate commonality of outlook among various cultures in regard to nearly every aspect of our comparative studies. In each case we find a predictable matching set of cosmological themes and concepts linked to a specific set of civilizing skills. In each culture, these are expressed through a coherent set of symbols whose definitions are founded on a common set of interpretive principles. In each culture, emphasis is placed on a common set of astronomical bodies and structures and on ritual shrines built on a common plan that often shares a very specific method of alignment. We see that the tradition moves through its aniconic and iconic stages in parallel from culture to culture, often with specific transpositions of symbolism occurring in matching ways during the same eras across multiple cultures.

In the earliest stages of the tradition we see great commonality of word forms and terminology, to such an extent that in *China's Cosmological Prehistory* we were able to use Dogon and Egyptian dictionaries to improve our understanding of ancient Chinese words. But we can also see that this commonality of language diverged somewhat over time and within different cultures. We also see that certain archaic word forms may have survived in Turkey and India, while more modernized pronunciations carried forward in places like ancient Egypt. Meanwhile, the Dogon dictionary presents us with an interesting intermixture of archaic and modernized word forms, and so serves as a referential link between the two.

Together, these shared aspects of the tradition lead us to a coherent set of commonly shared esoteric concepts that also cross cultures, such as the nature of how the universe formed or how matter emerges. In case after case, we have been able to illustrate ways in which these kinds of concepts were similarly understood by the various cultures we are studying. Perhaps the most tangible demonstration of the common origin of these traditions is found in these shared perspectives on creation, which, if scientifically accurate, could only be the end product of a systemized cosmology and reflective of positive knowledge on the part of some organized group in ancient times. That is especially true when fundamentals of the perspective rest on aspects of an astronomical body that cannot be readily seen, such as the massive dwarf star Sirius B or the effectively invisible spiral of Barnard's Loop. Such observational difficulties effectively rule out any credible suggestion of parallel development.

In the end, we can trace a credible lineage for our tradition that starts at Gobekli Tepe and carries forward in ways that are consistent with each of the later cultures we have studied. At Gobekli Tepe we find a blending of structural and symbolic elements that could have sensibly spawned what we see in each of the later traditions. Language comparisons support this view. A comparison of matching symbols and their known symbolism in the later cultures supports this view. Ancient textual references to an archaic point of origin, described in ways that are consonant with what we see at Gobekli Tepe, support this view. In other words, the sanctuary at Gobekli Tepe provides us with a reasonable, centrally situated point of origin for the various traditions we have explored in Africa, Egypt, India, Tibet, and China.

The main difficulty with that outlook is that it requires us to accept the related body of symbols, myths, words, and rituals as having been an instructed tradition. If we take that as a likely truth, then what we are ultimately left with are yet-unanswerable questions regarding the likely identity of the ancient instructors of that tradition.

Epilogue

The original concept for this book came to me in relation to the solitary phrase "point of origin." At the time, my sense was that the term had to do with tracing the various cultures I have explored in these studies back to a single common point of origin at Gobekli Tepe. However, as I pursued various avenues of research that arose in relation to the book, that same phrase, "point of origin," somehow kept turning up, cited again and again by the authors of a wide variety of references I was relying on as my primary sources.

For example, I discovered in the book *Sakti Cult in Orissa* that Francesco Brighenti, when discussing the outward spread of agriculture, language, and civilizing skills from a locale in western Iran nearby Gobekli Tepe, referred to that region as the "point of origin" of his Sakti cult. Adrian Snodgrass, when discussing the Buddhist concept of a sun door between the nonmaterial and material universes, which he located at the summit of the dome of the universe, described reaching that summit as arriving at "the point of origin" of the universe. Vulture Peak, the name given in Buddhism to the mythical domain in which knowledge was said to have been first transmitted to humanity, was similarly defined as the "point of origin" of that tradition.

In the Bambara culture, discussion of the egg-of-the-world concept (similar to the one held by the Dogon) defines the spiraling egg with the term Faro, which we take to be a likely correlate to the Egyptian term *pharaoh.* This is also the name given to the hub of the spiral, which is situated at the center of the egg, the same position that is held by the Dogon god Amma. When referring to this point, the Bambara say that it "constantly takes the point of origin." According to their tradition, the spiral represents "the displacement of Faro for the realization of all things in the universe."

There is an Egyptian concept that I take as a correlate to the phrase "point of origin." It is expressed by the word *bet,* which Budge defines as "the original place, the old home" and spells using the archaic vulture glyph.[1] It appears to be an archaic form, but its glyphs center on all the familiar symbols we associate with the spiraling egg of the world and the formation of mass or matter. A second word pronounced *bet* means "to shine," and so upholds the Bambara notion that this tiny spiral of matter involves a coil of mass that is entwined with light. The implication is that, at the eighth stage, in which this bubble-like egg bursts, light is a by-product. In the familiar domain of our material world there is a likely correlate to this, reflected in a concept called sonoluminescence. Reseachers have found that if they use a standing sound wave to form a bubble underwater, for reasons unknown light is emitted when the bubble bursts. So our discussion comes to an altogether fitting end by potentially pointing us to light's likely point of origin.

Notes

INTRODUCTION

1. Johnson, *Oriental Religions,* 44–45.

CHAPTER 1.
THE ANCIENT COSMOLOGICAL/
CIVILIZING PLAN

1. Dieterlen, *La Religion Bambara,* 40–41.
2. Budge, *Egyptian Hieroglyphic Dictionary,* 272b.
3. Ibid., 133b.
4. Ibid., 881b.
5. Ibid., 834a.

CHAPTER 2.
SYMBOLIC CONSTRUCTS OF
THE COSMOLOGY

1. Berriman, *Historical Metrology,* see index entry for cubits, 217.
2. Budge, *Egyptian Hieroglyphic Dictionary,* 20ab.
3. Snodgrass, *Symbolism of the Stupa,* 20.

CHAPTER 3.
CONSTRUCTS OF THE LANGUAGE OF COSMOLOGY

1. Scranton, *Sacred Symbols,* 114.
2. Budge, *Egyptian Hieroglyphic Dictionary,* 40b.

CHAPTER 4.
GOBEKLI TEPE AND ZEP TEPI

1. Dietrich, "Gobekli Tepe."
2. Budge, *Egyptian Hieroglyphic Dictionary,* 596a.
3. Clark, *Myth and Symbol,* 263–64.
4. Budge, *Egyptian Hieroglyphic Dictionary,* 830a.
5. Ibid., 828a.
6. Ibid., 661a.
7. Ibid., 664a.
8. Ibid., 878b.
9. Ibid., 836a.
10. Ibid., 878a.
11. Ibid.
12. Ibid., 834a.
13. Ibid., 835b.
14. Ibid., 834a.
15. Ibid., 835a.
16. Ibid., 879a.
17. Ibid., 837a.
18. Ibid., 294b.
19. Ibid., 295a.
20. Calame-Griaule, *Dictionnaire Dogon,* 292.
21. Budge, *Egyptian Hieroglyphic Dictionary,* 378b.
22. Ibid., 756a.
23. Ibid., 909a.
24. Ibid., 378b.
25. Calame-Griaule, *Dictionnaire Dogon,* 266.

CHAPTER 5.
ARCHAIC TEMPLE NAMES

1. Budge, *Egyptian Hieroglyphic Dictionary,* cxliv.
2. Ibid., 800a.
3. Ibid., 891a.
4. Ibid., 236ab.
5. Fairservis, *Roots of Ancient India,* 380.
6. Budge, *Egyptian Hieroglyphic Dictionary,* 43b.
7. Snodgrass, *Symbolism of the Stupa,* 315.
8. Narain, "Ganeśa," 29.
9. Ibid., 34.
10. Ibid., 25.
11. Beer, *Encyclopedia of Tibetan Symbols,* 82.
12. Budge, *Egyptian Hieroglyphic Dictionary,* 804a.
13. Mark Pagel, "Ultraconserved Words Point to Deep Language Ancestry across Eurasia," PNAS Early Edition, www.academia.edu/3703630/_PNAS_Ultraconserved_words_and_Eurasiatic_The_faces_in_the_fire_of_language_prehistory (accessed August 19, 2014).
14. Calame-Griaule, *Dictionnaire Dogon,* 231.
15. Budge, *Egyptian Hieroglyphic Dictionary,* 545b–48b.

CHAPTER 6.
TURKISH AND ARCHAIC WORD FORMS

1. Budge, *Egyptian Hieroglyphic Dictionary,* 211b.
2. Ibid.
3. Snodgrass, *Symbolism of the Stupa,* 287.
4. Budge, *Egyptian Hieroglyphic Dictionary,* 160a.
5. Ibid., 522b.
6. Ibid., 23a.
7. Ibid., 800b.
8. Ibid., 803a.
9. Ibid., 806a.

10. Calame-Griaule, *Dictionnaire Dogon,* 88–90.

11. Budge, *Egyptian Hieroglyphic Dictionary,* 800a.

12. Roger Blench, "Reports on Field Research: A Survey of Dogon Languages in Mali; Overview," Foundation for Endangered Languages, www.ogmios.org/ogmios_files/266.htm (accessed August 19, 2014).

CHAPTER 7.
THE SAKTI CULT IN ORISSA

1. Payne, *Saktas,* 6–7.

2. Brighenti, *Sakti Cult in Orissa,* 28.

3. Ibid., 231.

4. Ibid., 175.

5. Yuvra Krishan, "The Origins of Ganeśa," Artibus Asiae Publishers, 1981–82, www.jstor.org/stable/3249845 (accessed August 19, 2014).

6. Brighenti, *Sakti Cult in Orissa,* 341.

7. Ibid., 31.

8. Ibid., 16, 32.

9. Ibid., 32, 61.

10. Ibid., 297.

11. Ibid., 29.

12. Mitra, *Buddhist Monuments.* Mitra, D. (1971). *Buddhist Monuments.* Sahitya Samsad: Calcutta.

13. Brighenti, *Sakti Cult in Orissa,* 298.

14. Ibid., 46.

15. Ibid., 342.

16. Ibid., 35.

17. Ibid., 301.

18. Ibid., 20.

19. Ibid., 303.

20. Ibid., 37, 44.

21. Ibid., 38.

22. Ibid., 39.

23. Ibid., 288–89.

24. Ibid., 17.

25. Ibid., 18–19.

26. Ibid., 64.

27. Ibid., 32.

CHAPTER 8.
SAKTI REFERENCES IN ANCIENT EGYPT

1. Brighenti, *Sakti Cult in Orissa,* 34; Payne, *Saktas,* 7.

2. Payne, *Saktas,* 8.

3. Snodgrass, *Symbolism of the Stupa,* 211.

4. Budge, *Egyptian Hieroglyphic Dictionary,* 255–56.

5. Brighenti, *Sakti Cult in Orissa,* 59.

6. Budge, *Egyptian Hieroglyphic Dictionary,* 641a.

7. Ibid., 25a.

8. Ibid., 854a.

9. Ibid., 217a.

10. Brighenti, *Sakti Cult in Orissa,* 32.

11. Ibid., 294.

12. Budge, *Egyptian Hieroglyphic Dictionary,* 585b.

13. Ibid., 819b.

14. Ibid., 584a.

15. Ibid., 583b.

CHAPTER 9.
ASCENSION

1. Budge, *Egyptian Hieroglyphic Dictionary,* 646b.

2. Ibid., 524b.

3. Ibid., 12b, 14a.

4. Griaule and Dieterlen, *Pale Fox,* 187.

5. Scranton, *Sacred Symbols,* 140.

6. Snodgrass, *Symbolism of the Stupa,* 269–70.

7. Ibid., 275–76.

8. Ibid., 276–77.

9. Finegan, *Archeology of World Religions,* 191, 202–3.

10. Kaku, *Parallel Worlds,* 15.

11. Greene, *Hidden Reality,* 164.

12. Brighenti, *Sakti Cult in Orissa,* 488.

CHAPTER 10.
THE CONCEPT OF UNTYING

1. Budge, *Egyptian Hieroglyphic Dictionary,* 43b.

2. Ibid., 99a.

3. Ibid., 99b.

4. Ibid., 178ab.

5. Ibid., 296a.

6. Ibid., 401a.

7. Ibid., 630b.

8. Ibid., 665b.

9. Snodgrass, *Symbolism of the Stupa,* 286–98.

CHAPTER 11.
THE HELIACAL RISE OF SIRIUS

1. Saggs, *Civilization before Greece and Rome,* 230.

2. Clark, *Myth and Symbol,* 264.

3. Schwaller de Lubicz, *Sacred Science,* 27.

4. Budge, *Egyptian Hieroglyphic Dictionary,* 816a.

5. Calame-Griaule, *Dictionnaire Dogon,* 28.

6. Griaule and Dieterlen, *Pale Fox,* 279.

7. Quirke, *Ancient Egyptian Religion,* 93.

8. Calame-Griaule, *Dictionnaire Dogon,* 197; Budge, *Egyptian Hieroglyphic Dictionary,* 378b–79a.

9. Calame-Griaule, *Dictionnaire Dogon,* 260.

10. Jayaram V., "Zoroastrianism—The Old Iranian Calendars—Part 3," Hindu Website, www.hinduwebsite.com/zoroastrianism/calendar3.asp (accessed August 19, 2014).

CHAPTER 12.
ANCESTORS, DUAL ARMS, AND
THE CONCEPT OF THE EMBRACE

1. Budge, *Egyptian Hieroglyphic Dictionary,* 11b.

2. Ibid., 830a.

3. Ibid., 460a.

4. Ibid., 639a.

5. Ibid., 616b, 693a.

6. Ibid., 693a.

7. Ibid., 345a.

8. Calame-Griaule, *Dictionnaire Dogon,* 186.

9. Budge, *Egyptian Hieroglyphic Dictionary,* 879a.

10. Sanford, "Japan's Dual-Gaṇeśa Cult," 288–89.

11. Getty, *Ganesa,* 72–75.

12. Brown, *Ganesh,* 16.

13. Getty, *Ganesa,* 81.

14. Ibid., 84.

15. Norwood, "Symbols and Science," 278.

16. Budge, *Egyptian Hieroglyphic Dictionary,* 15b.

17. Ibid., 63b–64a.

18. Ibid., 252b.

19. Ibid., 317a.

20. Ibid., 317b.

21. Ibid., 463a.

22. Ibid., 479a.

23. Ibid., 772–73.

CHAPTER 13.
DEFINING A TEMPLE

1. Budge, *Egyptian Hieroglyphic Dictionary*, 453a.
2. Johnson, *Oriental Religions*, 799.
3. See www.isfahan.org.uk/glossary/gonbad/gonbad.html (accessed August 19, 2014).
4. Snodgrass, *Architecture, Time, and Eternity*, 124.
5. Budge, *Egyptian Hieroglyphic Dictionary*, 479a.
6. Ibid., 478b.
7. Ibid., 479a.
8. Griaule and Dieterlen, *Pale Fox*, 494.

CHAPTER 14.
THE BRIDGE OF SIRAH

1. Schwaller de Lubicz, *Egyptian Miracle*, 31.
2. Alam, Shah Manzoor, Dr. "Creation of Universe: Qur'anic Concepts and Scientific Theories," Imam Reza (A.S.) Network, www.imamreza .net/eng/imamreza.php?id=703 (accessed August 19, 2014).
3. Calame-Griaule, *Dictionnaire Dogon*, 244.
4. Ibid., 248.
5. David Bakst, "Cosmology of the Jewish Holy Days," www.cityofluz .com/wp-content/uploads/2014/04/Book-Body-of-Time.pdf.
6. Griaule and Dieterlen, *Pale Fox*, 82.
7. Budge, *Egyptian Hieroglyphic Dictionary*, 694–95.
8. David Bakst, "Cosmology of the Jewish Holy Days," www.chazonhato rah.org/uploads/file/Book-Body of Time.pdf.
9. Snodgrass, *Symbolism of the Stupa*, 211.
10. Ibid., 209.
11. Snodgrass, *Architecture, Time, and Eternity*, 356.

CHAPTER 15.
THE COSMOLOGICAL ROLE OF GANESHA

1. Getty, *Ganesa, xv–xvii.*
2. Ibid., 39.
3. Granoff, "Ganeśa as Metaphor," 88.
4. Budge, *Egyptian Hieroglyphic Dictionary,* 800a.
5. Ibid., cxii.
6. Ibid., 864a.
7. Ibid., 680b.
8. Ibid., 583–84.
9. Ibid., 4a.
10. Ibid., 4b.
11. Ibid., 19a, 117b.
12. Ibid., 117b.
13. Ibid., 646b.
14. Ibid., 615b.
15. Ibid., 583a.
16. Ibid., 419b.
17. Snodgrass, *Symbolism of the Stupa,* 287.
18. Budge, *Egyptian Hieroglyphic Dictionary,* 743b.
19. Ibid., 744a.
20. Ibid., 754.
21. Ibid., 704b.
22. Scranton, *Sacred Symbols,* 59; Budge, *Egyptian Hieroglyphic Dictionary,* 694b–95a.
23. Krishnaswami, *Broken Tusk,* 2.

CHAPTER 16.
ELEPHANTINE, THE NILE INUNDATION, AND THE GOD HAPY

1. Schwaller de Lubicz, *Sacred Science,* 109.
2. Quirke, *Ancient Egyptian Religion,* 73.

3. See the Deutsches Archäologisches Institut, www.dainst.org/en/project/ elephantin?ft=all (accessed October 21, 2014).

4. Hart, *Dictionary of Egyptian Gods and Goddesses,* 191.

5. Pritchard, *Ancient Near Eastern Texts,* 31.

6. Budge, *Egyptian Hieroglyphic Dictionary,* 507b.

7. Ibid., 467b.

8. Quirke, *Ancient Egyptian Religion,* 50.

9. Schwaller de Lubicz, *Sacred Science,* 177.

10. Budge, *Egyptian Hieroglyphic Dictionary,* 477b.

11. Quirke, *Ancient Egyptian Religion,* 50.

12. Dreyer, *Drei archaisch-hieratische Gefassaufschriften mit Jahresnamen auf Elephantine,* 98–109.

13. Budge, *Egyptian Hieroglyphic Dictionary,* 19a.

14. Ibid.

15. Scranton, *Sacred Symbols,* 59.

CHAPTER 17.
TAMIL WORD FORMS

1. Scranton, *Science of the Dogon,* 118.

CHAPTER 18.
A RATIONALE FOR THE CIVILIZING PLAN

1. Snodgrass, *Symbolism of the Stupa,* 3.

EPILOGUE

1. Budge, *Egyptian Hieroglyphic Dictionary,* 226b.

Bibliography

Beer, Robert. *The Encyclopedia of Tibetan Symbols and Motifs.* Boston: Shambhala, 1999.

Berriman, A. E. *Historical Metrology: A New Analysis of the Archaeological and the Historical Evidence Relating to Weights and Measures.* Westport, Conn.: Greenwood Press, 1969.

Brighenti, Francesco. *Sakti Cult in Orissa.* New Delhi: D. K. Printworld (P) Ltd., 1963.

Brown, Robert L., ed. *Ganesh: Studies of an Asian God.* Delhi, India: Sri Satguru Publications, 1991.

Budge, E. A. Wallis. *An Egyptian Hieroglyphic Dictionary.* New York: Dover Publications, Inc., 1978.

Calame-Griaule, Genevieve. *Dictionnaire Dogon.* Paris: Librarie C. Klincksieck, 1968.

Clark, R. T. Rundle. *Myth and Symbol in Ancient Egypt.* New York: Grove Press, 1960. First published, London: Thames and Hudson, 1959.

Dieterlen, Germaine. *La Religion Bambara.* Paris: Presses Universitaires de France, 1951.

Dietrich, Oliver. "Gobekli Tepe: A Stone Age Ritual Center in Southeastern Turkey." *Actual Archeology Magazine.* Summer 2012, 32–51.

Dreyer, Gunter. *Drei archaisch-hieratische Gefassaufschriften mit Jahresnamen auf Elephantine.* Wiesbaden, Germany: Festschrift Fecht, 1987.

Elwin, Verrier. *Tribal Myths of Orissa.* London: Oxford University Press, 1954.

Fairservis, Walter A., Jr. *The Roots of Ancient India*. New York: The MacMillan Company, 1971.

Finegan, Jack. *The Archeology of World Religions*. Princeton, N.J.: Princeton University Press, 1952.

Getty, Alice. *Ganesa: A Monograph on the Elephant-Faced God*. New Delhi: Pilgrim's Publishing, 2006.

Granoff, Phyllis. "Ganeśa as Metaphor: The *Mudgala Purāna*." In *Ganesh: Studies of an Asian God*, edited by Robert L. Brown, 85–100. Delhi, India: Sri Satguru Publications, 1991.

Greene, Brian. *The Hidden Reality: Parallel Universes and the Deep Laws of the Cosmos*. New York: Alfred A. Knopf, 2011.

Griaule, Marcel. *Conversations with Ogotemmeli*. Oxford, England: Oxford University Press, 1970.

Griaule, Marcel, and Germaine Dieterlen. *The Pale Fox*. Paris: Continuum Foundation, 1986.

Hagan, Helene. *The Shining Ones: An Entymological Essay on the Amazigh Roots of Egyptian Civilization*. Bloomington, Ind.: Xlibris, 2000.

Hart, George. *A Dictionary of Egyptian Gods and Goddesses*. London and New York: Routledge, 1999.

He Pingzheng. *Naxi Dongba Pictograph Dictionary*. Kunming, China: Yunnan Fine Arts Publishing House, 2004.

Iyengar, T. R. Sesha. *Ancient Dravidians*. Chennai, India: MJP Publishers, 2007.

Johnson, Samuel. *Oriental Religions and Their Relation to Universal Religion*. Boston: James R. Osgood and Company, 1872.

Kaku, Michio. *Parallel Worlds: A Journey through Creation, Higher Dimensions, and the Future of the Cosmos*. New York: Doubleday, 2005.

Krishnaswami, Uma. *The Broken Tusk: Stories of the Hindu God Ganesha*. Little Rock, Ark.: August House Publishers, 2006.

Mathieu, Christine. *A History and Anthropological Study of the Ancient Kingdoms of the Sino-Tibetan Borderland—Naxi and Mosuo*. Lewiston, Australia: The Edwin Mellen Press, 2003.

Mitchiner, John E. *Traditions of the Seven Rsis*. Delhi, India: Motalil Banarsidass Publishers Private Limited, 1982. Reprinted in 2000.

Mitra, Debala. *Buddhist Monuments.* Calcutta, India: Sahitya Samsad, 1971.

Narain, A. K. "Gaṇeśa: A Protohistory of the Idea and the Icon." In *Ganesh: Studies of an Asian God,* edited by Robert L. Brown, 19–48. Delhi, India: Sri Satguru Publications, 1991.

Norwood, J. W. "Symbols and Science." *New Age Magazine* 18 (1913). Published by the Supreme Council of the 33rd Degree A. & A. Scottish Rite.

Payne, Ernest A. *The Saktas: An Introductory and Comparative Study.* Calcutta, India: Munshiram Manoharlal Publishers Pvt. Ltd., 1997.

Pritchard, James B. *Ancient Near Eastern Texts Relating to the Old Testament.* 3rd ed. Princeton, N.J.: Princeton University Press, 1969.

Quirke, Stephen. *Ancient Egyptian Religion.* Mineola, N.Y.: Dover Publications, 1997.

Rock, Joseph. *A Na-Khi–English Encyclopedic Dictionary, Part I.* Rome: Istituto Italiano per il Medio ed Estremo Oriente, 1963.

Saggs, H. W. E. *Civilization before Greece and Rome.* New Haven, Conn.: Yale University Press, 1989.

Sanford, James H. "Literary Aspects of Japan's Dual-Gaṇeśa Cult." In *Ganesh: Studies of an Asian God,* edited by Robert L. Brown, 287–335. Delhi, India: Sri Satguru Publications, 1991.

Schwaller de Lubicz, R. A. *The Egyptian Miracle: An Introduction to the Wisdom of the Temple.* New York: Inner Traditions International, 1985.

———. *Sacred Science: The King of Pharaonic Theocracy.* New York: Inner Traditions International, 1982.

Scranton, Laird. *China's Cosmological Prehistory.* Rochester, Vt.: Inner Traditions, 2014.

———. *The Cosmological Origins of Myth and Symbol: From the Dogon and Ancient Egypt to India, Tibet, and China.* Rochester, Vt.: Inner Traditions, 2010.

———. "Revisiting Griaule's Dogon Cosmology: Comparative Cosmology Provides New Evidence to a Controversy." *Anthropology News,* April 2007. Published by the University of Chicago Press.

———. *Sacred Symbols of the Dogon: The Key to Advanced Science in the Ancient Egyptian Hieroglyphs.* Rochester, Vt.: Inner Traditions, 2006.

———. *The Science of the Dogon: Decoding the African Mystery Tradition.* Rochester, Vt.: Inner Traditions, 2007.

Snodgrass, Adrian. *Architecture, Time, and Eternity.* Delhi, India: Aditya Prakashan, 1990.

———. *The Symbolism of the Stupa.* Delhi, India: Motilal Banarsidass Publishers, 1992.

Wheatley, Paul. *The Pivot of the Four Quarters: A Preliminary Enquiry into the Origins and Character of the Ancient Chinese City.* Chicago: Aldine Publishing Company, 1971.

Witzel, E. J. Michael. *The Origins of the World's Mythologies.* New York: Oxford University Press, 2012.

Index

BOOKS OF RELATED INTEREST

China's Cosmological Prehistory
The Sophisticated Science Encoded in Civilization's Earliest Symbols
by Laird Scranton

The Science of the Dogon
Decoding the African Mystery Tradition
by Laird Scranton
Foreword by John Anthony West

The Velikovsky Heresies
Worlds in Collision and Ancient Catastrophes Revisited
by Laird Scranton

Gobekli Tepe: Genesis of the Gods
The Temple of the Watchers and the Discovery of Eden
by Andrew Collins
Introduction by Graham Hancock

Black Genesis
The Prehistoric Origins of Ancient Egypt
by Robert Bauval and Thomas Brophy, Ph.D.

Forgotten Civilization
The Role of Solar Outbursts in Our Past and Future
by Robert M. Schoch, Ph.D.

The 12th Planet
by Zecharia Sitchin

The Lost Book of Enki
Memoirs and Prophecies of an Extraterrestrial God
by Zecharia Sitchin

INNER TRADITIONS • BEAR & COMPANY
P.O. Box 388
Rochester, VT 05767
1-800-246-8648
www.InnerTraditions.com

Or contact your local bookseller